The place names of Middlesex (inclucing those parts of the county of London formerly contained within the boundaries of the old county)

J E. B. b. 1894 Gover

THE PLACE NAMES OF MIDDLESEX

THE PLACE NAMES OF

MIDDLESEX

(INCLUDING THOSE PARTS OF THE COUNTY OF LONDON FORMERLY CONTAINED WITHIN THE BOUNDARIES OF THE OLD COUNTY)

BY

J. E. B. GOVER, B.A. (Cantab.)

LONGMANS, GREEN AND CO.

39 PATERNOSTER ROW, LONDON, E.C. 4

NEW YORK, TORONTO

BOMBAY, CALCUTTA AND MADRAS

1922

PREFACE.

As a student of place name etymology, I have been struck by the fact that, whereas many of our northern and midland counties have been ably dealt with by competent hands, the southern counties, especially those in the vicinity of London, have for the most part been left untouched. It is for this reason that I have undertaken the present work. I selected Middlesex for my subject—first, because it is a small county, and an investigation into the sources of its names could be accomplished in a shorter time than would be possible with one of the other " home counties "; and secondly, because it contains the greatest city in the world, and in consequence might invoke more general interest than would be the case with any ordinary county.

I take the opportunity of thanking Professor Mawer of Liverpool University for valuable help and advice on the subject which he has given me both personally and through the medium of his recent article on " English Place Name Study " printed by the British Academy, and which has lessened my diffidence in offering this work to the public. I also desire to acknowledge my indebtedness to my father, Mr. J. M. Gover, K.C., for assistance in revising proofs and otherwise.

J. E. B. G.

LONDON, *May*, 1922.

INTRODUCTION.

In an attempt to elucidate the meanings of the place names of Middlesex, I have tried, to the best of my ability, to follow out the rules laid down by Professor Skeat, Professor Mawer, Professor Wyld and others. That is to say, I have first collected all available old spellings from the various records (of which a list will be found on pages xi-xiv); and secondly, having stated these in chronological order, I have endeavoured to interpret their meaning, paying strict attention in every case to the usual sound laws, and also to the topographical situation of the places in question.

Although Middlesex is the smallest but one of our English counties, I have found my task by no means free from difficulty. No good County History of Middlesex exists to my knowledge (only one volume of the Victoria Series having been published, and that, curiously enough, being the second volume); and although Lysons covers the ground fairly completely in his "Environs of London," he occasionally gives wrong references, and his attempted etymologies must in all cases be accepted with great caution.

Since the coming of the railways in the nineteenth century the growth of London has been amazing.

Originally occupying roughly the district now known as "the City," it had grown very little outward at the time of the Great Fire. Even as recently as 100 years ago the town hardly extended further west than Hyde Park or further north than the present Marylebone, Euston and City roads. Now the streets are stretching further out every year, and at the present rate of advance it appears probable that the whole county will be converted into metropolitan suburb at no distant date.

The scope of this book is to include the names of all places historically and topographically in Middlesex, but excluding the actual "City" names, which have been ably treated by Mr. Henry A. Harben in his "Dictionary of London," published in 1918. I have, however, taken the liberty of including a few names such as Aldgate, Gracechurch, Walbrook, etc., which I consider to be proper "place names" and such as may be fairly included in the original county of Middlesex. I have also entered many place names now extinct or vanished, considering them to be as interesting to the philologist as those still surviving, together with a few names of historical or modern origin, a consideration of which, though of little interest from a language point of view, may tend to reassure investigators, who might otherwise be speculating on the chances of "folk etymology" in such names as Copenhagen, Maida Vale, Portobello, etc.

It will be noticed that I have not attempted any disquisition on the subject of Place Name Study as a whole. I considered it unnecessary since this has already been ably and learnedly dealt with by such eminent authorities as the late Professor Skeat and others.

My aim has been simply to add to the present list of county monographs on the subject a contribution on the local names of the County of Middlesex, comparing these, whenever possible, with names in other English counties, in the Anglo-Saxon Charters, and especially in Kemble's "Codex Diplomaticus," which contains a complete index in the final volume.

BIBLIOGRAPHY.

I. GENERAL SOURCES.

Abbreviations.

A Descriptive Catalogue of Ancient Deeds. (Public Record Office.) 6 vols. 1890- . . . . . A.D.

Cartularium Saxonicum. By W. de G. Birch. 3 vols. 1885, 1887, 1893 . . . . Bch.

Calendarium Rotulorum Chartarum. 1803 . . . Cal. Rot. Ch.

Calendarium Rotulorum Patentium in turri Londiniensi. 1802 . . . . Cal. Rct. P.

Calendar of Charter Rolls (1226-1447). Public Record Office. 5 vols. 1903- . . . . . . Ch.

Two of the Saxon Chronicles Parallel. 2 vols. Ed. Plummer and Earle. Oxford, 1892-1899 . . . Chron.

Calendar of the Close Rolls (1227-1385). Public Record Office. 29 vols. 1892- . . . . . Close.

Crawford Charters. Ed. Napier and Stevenson. Oxford, 1895 . . . . Crawford.

Domesday Book. 3 vols. Record Commission. 1816 . Dd.

Monasticon Anglicanum. 6 vols. Ed. Dugdale. 1846 . Dug.

A Handbook of the Land Charters and other Saxonic Documents. Ed. J. Earle. 1888 . . . . Earle.

Calendarium inquisitionum post-mortem sive Escaetarum. 4 vols. From 1806 . . . . . Escaet.

Excerpta e rotulis finium in turri Londiniensi asservati, tempore regis Johannis. Record Commission. T. D. Hardy. 1835 . . . . Excerpta.

Inquisitions and Assessments Relating to Feudal Aids. 5 vols. Public Record Office. 1899- . . . F.A.

Book of Fees, commonly called Testa de Nevill: Reformed . . . by the Deputy Keeper of the Records. Part I. 1920 . . . . Fees.

BIBLIOGRAPHY

Abbreviations.

Calendar of the Fine Rolls. 5 vols. Public Record Office. 1911- . . . . Fine.

Gesta Abbatum Monasterii Sancti Albani. Ed. H. T. Riley. 3 vols. 1867 . . . . . Gesta.

Rotuli Hundredorum, temp. Henry III. and Edward I. 2 vols. 1812 . . . . . . H.R.

Index to the Charters and Rolls in the British Museum. 2 vols. Ed. Ellis and Bickley, 1900-1912 . . Ind.

Calendarium . . . inquisitionum ad quod damnum. 1803 . . . . I.D.

Calendar of Inquisitions post-mortem. 11 vols. Public Record Office. 1904 . . . . . I.p.m.

Calendar of Inquisitions Miscellaneous (Chancery). 2 vols. Public Record Office . . . . I.M.

Codex Diplomaticus. 6 vols. Ed. J. Kemble. London, 1839-1848 . . . . . . Kble.

Public Record Office Lists and Indexes. 45 vols. . L.I.

Letters and Papers of the Reign of Henry VIII. 21 vols. Vols. 1-4, ed. Brewer; Vols. 5-21, ed. Gairdner. . L.P.H.

Magnum Rotulum Scaccarii vel magnum rotulum pipae. Ed. J. Hunter . . . . . . M.R.

Nonarum Inquisitionis in Curia Scaccarii (temp. regis Edwardi III.). 1807 . . . . . N.I.

Calendar of Patent Rolls. 55 vols. Public Record Office. 1891- . . . . Pat.

Placitorum in domo capitulari Westmonasteriensi asservatorum Abbreviatio. 1818 . . . . Plac. Abb.

Placitorum de quo Warranto. 1818 . . . . Pl.W.

Pipe Roll Society Publications. Record Commission. 37 vols., covering 1158-1199 . . . . . P.R.

Calendar of the Proceedings in Chancery in the Reign of Queen Elizabeth. 3 vols. 1830 . . . . Proc. Chanc.

Rotulorum originalium in curia Scaccarii Abbreviatio 2 vols. 1810 . . . . Rot. Abb.

Rotulus Cancellarii vel Antigraphum magni rotuli pipae (de tertio anno regni regis Johannis) . . . , Rot. Canc.

Rotuli Chartarum in turri Londiniensi asservati. Vol. I., pars I. 1837 . . . . . . Rot. Chart.

Red Book of the Exchequer. 3 vols. Ed. Hubert Hall, F.S.A. 1896 . . . . R.E.

	Abbreviations.
Rotuli curiae regis. 2 vols. Ed. Sir F. Palgrave. 1835	Rot. C.R.
Rotuli Litterarum clausarum in turri Londiniensi asservati. 2 vols. 1844	Rot. L.C.
Rotuli Litterarum Patentium in turri Londiniensi asservati. Vol. I., pars I. (Record Commission. 1835)	Rot. L.P.
Rotuli de oblatis et finibus in turri Londiniensi asservati, tempore regis Johannis. (Record Commission. T. D. Hardy). 1835	Rot. O.F.
Onomasticon Anglo-Saxonicum. A list of Anglo-Saxon proper names from the time of Beda to that of King John. Ed. W. G. Searle. Cambridge, 1897 . .	Searle.
Selden Society Publications. 38 vols. . . .	S.S.
Taxatio Ecclesiastica Angliae et Walliae auctoritate Papae Nicholas IV. Circa A.D. 1291	T.E.
Diplomatarium Anglicum aevi Saxonici. Ed. B. Thorpe. London, 1865	Thorpe.
Testa de Nevill sive Liber Feodorum in curia Scaccarii (temp. Henry III. and Edward I.) . . .	T.N.
Valor Ecclesiasticus. c. 1535. 6 vols. . . .	V.E.

II. SPECIAL SOURCES OF MIDDLESEX NAMES.

London and Middlesex Archæological Society Transactions. London, 1860, etc.	Arch.
London, North of the Thames. By Sir Walter Besant .	Besant.
Calendar of Coroner's Rolls of the City of London. Ed. Reginald Sharpe. London, 1913 . . .	Cor.
A Calendar of the Feet of Fines for London and Middlesex. 2 vols. Ed. W. J. Hardy, F.S.A., and W. Page, F.S.A. London, 1892-1893 . . .	F.F.
Greater London, a Narrative of its History, its People, and its Places. Vol. I. Ed. Edward Walford .	G.L.
A Dictionary of London. By Henry A. Harben, F.S.A. London, 1918	Harben.
Environs of London. By Rev. Daniel Lysons. 4 vols. and Supplement. London, 1792 . . .	Lysons.
Memorials of St. John at Hackney. By R. Simpson .	Mem.
Old and New London. 6 vols. By Walter Thornbury .	O. and N.
Stow's Survey of London, 1603. Ed. C. L. Kingsford, M.A. 2 vols.	Stow.

The Victoria History of the County of Middlesex. Ed.
  William Page. Vol. II. London, 1911 . . . V.C.H.
Middlesex Pedigrees. Harleian Society Publications.
  Vol. LXV. 1914 . . . . Mid. Ped.

Abbreviations.

III. MONOGRAPHS ON ENGLISH PLACE AND PERSONAL NAMES.

Alexander, H. . Place Names of Oxfordshire. 1912.
Baddeley, W. St. C. ,, ,, Gloucestershire. 1913.
Bannister, A. T. . ,, ,, Herefordshire. 1916.
Duignan, W. H. . Notes on Staffordshire Place Names. 1902.
  ,, . Warwickshire Place Names. 1912.
  ,, . Worcestershire ,, 1905.
Ekblom, E. . . Place Names of Wiltshire. 1907.
Goodall, A. . . ,, ,, S.W. Yorkshire. 1914.
Jackson, C. E. . ,, ,, Durham. 1916.
Johnston, J. B. . ,, ,, England and Wales. 1915.
  ,, . ,, ,, Scotland. 1903.
Joyce, P. W. . . Origin and History of Irish Names of Places.
  2 series. 1870, 1875.
Mawer, Allen . . Place Names of Northumberland and Durham.
  1920.
  ,, . . English Place Name Study, its present condition
  and future possibilities. (Proc. Brit. Acad.
  Vol. X.) 1921.
McClure, Edmund . British Place Names in their historical setting.
  1910.
Middendorff, H. . Altenglisches Flurnamenbuch. 1902.
Moore, A. W. . . Manx Names. 1903.
Moorman, F. W. . Place Names of the West Riding of Yorks. 1910.
Morgan, T. . . Place Names of Wales. 1912.
Mutschmann, H. . ,, ,, Nottinghamshire. 1913.
Roberts, R. G. . ,, ,, Sussex. 1914.
Skeat, W. W. . . ,, ,, Bedfordshire. 1906.
  ,, . . ,, ,, Berkshire. 1911.
  ,, . . ,, ,, Cambridgeshire. 1901.
  ,, . . ,, ,, Hertfordshire. 1904.
  ,, . . ,, ,, Huntingdonshire. 1902.
  ,, . . ,, ,, Suffolk. 1911.

Taylor, J.	. .	Words and Places. (Revised edition. 1911.)
Walker, B.	. .	Place Names of Derbyshire. 1914-1915.
Weekley, E.	. .	Romance of Names. Pp. 96-142. 1914.
„	. .	Surnames. Pp. 47-101. 1916.
Wyld, H. C., and Hirst, T. O.		Place Names of Lancashire. 1911.
Zachrisson, R. E.	.	Anglo-Norman Influence on English Place Names. 1909.

IV. DICTIONARIES, Etc.

Bosworth	. .	An Anglo-Saxon Dictionary. Ed. Prof. Toller.
Bradley	. .	Middle English Dictionary. By F. H. Stratman, Revised by H. Bradley.
E.D.D.	. .	English Dialect Dictionary. 6 vols. 1898-1905. Ed. Joseph Wright.
N.E.D.	. .	New English Dictionary. Ed. A-V Inclusive. 1888, etc.
Skeat	. .	Etymological Dictionary of the English Language. Ed. Rev. W. W. Skeat, M.A. Fourth edition. 1910.

V. A LIST OF SOME USEFUL MAPS.

Camden	. .	(Map of Middlesex in Camden's Britannia.) 1695.
Greenwood	. .	Map of the County of Middlesex. By C. Greenwood. 2 inches = 1 mile. 1819.
Rocque	. .	A Topographical Map of the County of Middlesex. By J. Rocque. 4 sheets. 1754.
Seller	. .	The County of Middlesex actually surveyed by John Seller. 1710.
Speed	. .	An Atlas of England and Wales. By J. Speed. 1610.

Also map in Norden's "Speculum Britanniæ" (1596), of which Speed's is a mere augmentation.

ETYMOLOGICAL REFERENCES.

A.S. = Anglo-Saxon (Old English).
M.E. = Middle English.
O.N. = Old Norse.

The sign (‡) before a name means that the charter from which it is taken is a later copy of a lost original. Hence these names are often not A.S. but M.E. in form.

KEY TO PHONETIC SYMBOLS USED IN THIS BOOK.

VOWELS.		CONSONANTS.	
Symbol.	*Key Word.*	*Symbol.*	*Key Word*
æ	bat.	b	bat.
aː	bath.	k	cat.
ε	bet.	d	dad.
εː	Baring.	f	fat.
eɪ ‡	bane.	g	gap.
ə	butter.	h	hat.
əː	bird.	l	late.
ɪ	bit.	m	mate.
ɪː	bee.	n	net.
ɔ	box.	p	pet.
ɔː	ball.	r	red.
ou ‡	boat.	s	said.
u	bull.	t	ten.
uː	boon.	v	vein.
ʌ	but.	w	wind.
aɪ	bite.	z	wise.
au	bough.	j	yes.
ɔɪ	boil.	ʃ	shop.
		ʒ	azure.
		θ	thigh.
		ð	thy.
		ŋ	king.
		x	(Scotch) night.

‡ As pronounced in the South of England.

MIDDLESEX PLACE NAMES ARRANGED ALPHABETICALLY.

An asterisk (*) before a name denotes that the place is not found in present-day maps.

ABCHURCH (in the City).
- *c.* 1198.   Abechurch (quoted Harben).
- 1228.   Abbecherche (A.D.).
- 1291.   Abbechurch (T.E.).
- 1428.   Abbechirche (F.A.).
- 1565.   Abchurch (F.F.).

Prefix is an A.S. personal name Aba or Abba, of which Searle gives several examples.

Cf. *Abinger, Abingdon, Abington,* etc. in various counties.

ACTON.
- 1210.   Actone (R.E.).
- 1216-1307 ⎫
- 1291   ⎬ Acton ⎰ (T.N.).
- 1316   ⎭   ⎱ (T.E.).
                    (F.A.).
- 1316.   Aketon (Ch.).

Acton in the F.F. *passim.*

"oak farm or enclosure."   A.S. *ác tún.

The vowel is shortened in composition before *ct.*

ALDERMANBURY (in the City).
- *c.* 1190.   Aldermanesbury (A.D.).
- 1202.   Aldermannesbir' (Rot. Canc.).
- 1267.   Aldermanbury (Escaet),

1

" stronghold or manor of the 'alderman'." See p. 112.
A.S. *ealdorman* meant a " prince," " noble," " one of high
rank." See N.E.D.

ALDERSGATE (a City gate).

    c. 1000.   Ealdredesgate (quoted Harben).

1197		(F.F.).
1260	Aldredesgate	(A.D.).
1216-1307		(H.R.).

    1352.   Aldresgate (Escaet).

    1535.   Aldersgate (V.E.).

  Searle gives sixty-six examples of the A.S. personal name
" Ealdred."

ALDGATE (a City gate).

    1108.   Alegate (quoted Harben).

    1231.   Allegate (F.F.).

1268		(I.p.m.).
1272-1377	Alegate	(P.W.).
1291		(T.E.)

    1295, 1348.   Aldgate (F.F.).

1428	Algate	(F.A.).
1535		(V.E.).

    1618.   Aldgate (Stow's survey).

  The old forms show that the prefix is not A.S. *eald* " old,"
but a personal name Ala or Alla.

ALDWICH (Strand).

    1219.   Aldewich (F.F.).

    1233.   Aldewych (F.F.).

    1267.   Aldewich (Ch.).

* se ealda wíc, " the old dwelling or settlement."

  * Ealdan wíc, " dwelling of Ealda," is also possible.

ALPERTON.

> ? 1199. Alprinton (F.F.).
> 1200. Alperton (Rot. c.r.).
> 1322. Alpertone (Cor.).
> 1342. Apurton (F.F.).
> 1399. Alpurton (F.F.).
> 1407. Halperton (F.F.).
> 1508. Alperton (F.F.).

"farm or enclosure of Ealhperht"—for Ealhberht, the *b* becoming voiceless after the "h" (= χ). See *Epperston* in "Place Names of Notts," p. 48.

The earliest form looks like some other type, if referring to this place.

ASHFORD.

Type I.

> ‡ 1062. Exforde (Kble.).
> 1086 ⎫
> 1293 ⎭ Exeforde ⎰(Dd.). ⎱(I.p.m.).
> 1470. Ashford (Escaet).
> 1488, 1517. Assheford (F.F.).
> 1610. Asheford (Speed).

Type II.

> ‡ 969. Ecclesforde (Bch., Kble., Thorpe).
> 1291. Ethelesford (T.E.) [*t* clerical error for *c*].
> 1294. Echelesford (F.F.).
> 1272-1377 ⎫
> 1327-1377 ⎭ Echeleford ⎰(P.W.). ⎱(N.I.).
> 1535. Echelford (V.E.).

Type I. Prefix either A.S. *æsc* "ash" or Celtic root *esk, *eks = "water," as in river names Esk, Exe, Axe, etc.

Type II. Prefix is a personal name *Æccel*, diminutive of Æcce or Æcci (2 in Searle).

1*

* Astleham (Laleham).

    1291. Estelham (F.F.).
    1362. Hastelham (F.F.).
    1445. Astleham (Index).
    1517. Astelam (F.F.).
    1819. Astleham (Greenwood).

The A.S. *æstel* means "a waxen tablet" and could hardly fit in here. Perhaps a personal name * Eastel. Eastulf (Eastwulf) is the nearest name in Searle, and is possible (cf. Harlesden).

Barnet, Friern Barnet.

    1216-1307. la Bernete (H.R.).
    1237. Little Bernete (F.F.).
    1272-1377. la Bernette (P.W.).
    1325. Barnette (F.F.).
    1408. Barnet (F.F.).
    1460. Freron Barnet (L.I., vol. 12).
    1535. Freren Bñet, Friern Bñet (V.E.).
    1610. Fryarn Barnet (Speed).

Under *Chipping Barnet* (Herts), Prof. Skeat explained this name as Old French *bernette*, diminutive of *berne* "a slope, edge, bank"—of Teutonic origin and cognate with English "brim."

The place, therefore, is of post-conquest origin.

Friern Barnet was in the possession of the friars or brethren of the order of the priory of St. John of Jerusalem. M.E. frere > A.F. frere, freire "brother" survives in its original form in the surnames Frere, Freer.

Barnsbury.

    1406 } Bernersbury { (F.F.).
    1418 }   { (Escaet).
    1422. Berners Maner' in Iseldon (Escaet).

1492. Barnersbury (F.F.).
1541. Barnardesbury (F.F.).
1543. Barnesbury (F.F.).

" stronghold or manor of Bern(i)er."   See p. 99.

B. is a Norman personal name, cf. Ralph de Berners (ob. 1297) and Roger de Berners (F.F. anno. 1356).

BAYSWATER (Paddington).

c. 1400. Baynards Watering Place (quoted Besant).
1653. Baynards Watering (quoted O. and N.).
1710. Beards Watering Place (Seller).
1809. Byards Watering Place (quoted Besant).
1819. Bayswater (Greenwood).

Evidently a cut down form of the Norman personal name Baynard, Baignard (cf. "*Baynards*" in Surrey).   Possibly named after the B. mentioned in Dd. who held land in the demesne of the Church of St. Peter of Westminster, or after one of his descendants.

The " water" referred to is the Westbourne stream.

BEDFONT.

1086. Bedefunt, Bedefunde, West Bedefund (Dd.).
1199. Bedefunte (F.F.).
1200. Bedefunt (Rot. c.r.).
1210. Bedefont (R.E.).
1216-1307. Westbedefunte, Estbedefont (T.N.).
1428. Bedfount (F.A.).

" well or spring of Beda (Bæda)," cf. " the Venerable Bede."
A.S. font > Latin font-[fons].

BEETONSWOOD FARM (Ickenham).

Beeton's Wood marked in Rocque.   Probably an imported name.

BELSIZE (Hampstead).

So spelt in Norden and Rocque.   Belsyse in Speed.   Lysons also quotes forms Belses, Belseys of earlier date, and states that the place dates back to at least 1400 A.D.

French "*bel sis*," i.e. "beautifully situated," "finely placed."   Belsize House (demolished last century) was situated on the slopes of Hampstead, facing south.

BENTLEY PRIORY (Stanmore).

    1244.   Benetlega (S.S., vol. 15).
    1248.   Benethley, Benethleya (Dug.).
    1544.   Bentley (L.I., vol. 34).

The prefix is A.S. *beonet* " a kind of coarse grass," " bent grass."   There are many places of this name in England.

BETHNAL GREEN.

    13th century.   Blithehale (A.D.).
    1341.   Blithenhale (A.D.).
    1389.   Blythenhale (F.F.).
    1550.   Bleten hall green (quoted in Stow's survey, vol. 2).
    1568.   Bednalgrene (F.F.).
    1603.   Blethenhal green now called Bednal-greene (Stowe).
    1642.   Bethnal Green (Index).

A.S. æt ðám blíðan heale, " at the happy, pleasant ('blithe') nook or corner."   See *Hale* (*infra*).

Or *Bliða* may have been used as a personal name, short for Blithhelm, Blithhere, Blithmund, etc. (see *Searle*), this being perhaps the most likely sense.

Loss of one "l" by dissimilation.

BILLINGSGATE (in the City).

    c. 1100.   Billingesgate (quoted Harben).
    c. 1200.   Billynggesgate (A.D).

1291
1393 } Billingesgate { (T.E.).
1428 (Escaet).
(F.A.).

"gate of Billing," i.e. of the son of *Billa.*

A.S. *bil* "a kind of sword," "bill," was used as the first element of some personal names, like most "war words," cf. *Billingshurst* (Sussex).

BISHOPSGATE (in the City).

1086. ad portam episcopi (Dd.).
1216-1307. Bischopesgate (H.R.).
1232. Bissopegate (F.F.).
1291. Bissopisgate (T.E.), etc.

BLACKWALL (Poplar).

1377. Blakewale (quoted O. and N.).
1480. Black Wall (quoted O. and N.).
1541. Blackewall (S.S., vol. 8).
1610. Blackwall (Speed).

Referring to a wall along the Thames bank.

BLOOMSBURY.

c. 1272. Blemondisberi (A.D.).
1295. Blomundesbury (Escaet).
1324. Blemondesbiry (I.p.m.).
1535. Blumbesbury (V.E.).
1567. Blomesburye (F.F.).

"stronghold or manor of Bleomund." Probably named after the William Blemund, who held land in "Totenhale" (Tottenham Court) in 1202 (F.F.).

But the modern outcome is due to the type Blōm—as in the 1295 form.

Blemund (Bleomund ?) looks Teutonic, like most Old French names, $\sqrt{\text{mund}}$ = "protection," "protector."

Loss of medial syllable is regular, cf. *Harmondsworth* (*infra*).

BOSTON HOUSE (Ealing).

      1535.   Bordeston (V.E.).

      1695.   Boston (Camden).

" farm of Bord—or possibly Bordel," cf. *Bordesley* (Warwick), rs > rds, then loss of *r* possibly through influence of Boston (Lincs) since *Borstal* (Kent) retains it.

BOTWELL HOUSE (Hayes).

      ‡831.   Botewælle (Bch, Kble).

      1368.   Bodewell (F.F.).

      1480.   Bodwell (L.I., vol. 16).

      1754.   Botwell (Rocque).

" well or spring of Bota or Boda " (both in Searle).

BOURNE FARM (Harefield).

    Marked in Rocque. The 1-inch ordnance map shows a small stream flowing past it.

Bow.

      1279.   Stratford atte Bowe (F.F.).

      1346.   Stratford atte Boghe (F.F.).

      1349.   Strettford atte Bowe (Rot. abb.).

    c. 1386.   Stratford atte Bowe (Chaucer: Prol. Cant. Tales, line 125).

      1535.   Stratford at Bowe (V.E.).

      1754.   Bow (Rocque).

" ford at the street." " Street " here, as usually in place names, refers to a Roman road. " Atte " is M.E.; earlier form is *atten* from A.S. æt ðám (at the).

    Bow refers to the arched bridge built over the Lea here at the time of Henry I, and supposed to be the first of its kind in England.

    The name Stratford is now restricted to the nineteenth century town on the Essex side of the river, Bow being still retained for the district on the London (Middlesex) side.

BOWES PARK.

     1412.   (The manor of) Bowes (F.F.).

     1695.   Bowe farm (Camden).

     1710.   Bows farm (Seller).

Bowe or Bowes I take to be a man's name, perhaps originally from Bowes (Yorkshire), which was spelt Boues and Boghes in the thirteenth century, or else from *Bow* (*supra*). Or possibly the name may be local, like Bow, from an arched bridge over the little stream here, which runs into the Lea.

BRACKENBURY FARM (Ickenham).

     1485.   Brakenburgh (I.p.m.).

     1488.   Brakenborough (F.F.).

1558-1579.   Brakenbroughes (L.I., vol. 7).

Lysons says that this place took its name from a certain Thomas de Brakynburgh, anno 1350.

    There is a *Brackenborough* in Lincolnshire.

BREAKSPEARS (Harefield).

    Marked in Norden (1596). Called after a family *Brakespere*, cf. Nicholas Brakespere mentioned *re* Ruislip in 1246 (S.S., vol. 2). The meaning of this personal name is obvious, cf. *Shakespeare*.

BRENT (river).

     972.   Innan, of, brægentan (Bch.).

     978.   Brægenta (Index).

    1202.   Brainte (F.F.).

    1384.   Breynte (F.F.).

    1556.   Braynt (F.F.).

cf. also form as prefix in Brentford (*infra*) before twelfth century. The name of the river in A.S. spelling is *Brægent*, but it is probably Celtic or pre-Celtic.

    Johnston's derivations are unlikely, for Welsh gw > original Celtic w (u), not g.

BRENTFORD.

      705.   Breguntford (Index).

      780.   Bragentforda, Bregentforda, Breguntforde (Kble.).

      781.   Bregentforda (Earle).

   1016.   æt Brægentforda, æt Brentforda (Chron.).

   1222.   Brainford (F.F.).

   1291 } Breynford { (T.E.).
   1316 } Breynford { (F.A.).

   1340.   Braynford (Index).

   1428.   Brayneford (F.A.).

   1596.   Brentford (Norden).

"ford over the river Brent."

nf > ntf, the *t* being reintroduced through the influence of the river name, where it had been retained.

BROCKLEY HILL (Elstree).

   1596.   Brokeley Hill (Norden).

   1754.   Brockley Hill (Rocque).

As there is no appreciable stream near by, the prefix is possibly A.S. broc "badger."

BROMLEY (Bow) [brʌmlɪ].

   1203.   Brambeleg (F.F.).

c. 1220.   Brembeley (Index).

   1251.   Brombelleg (F.F.).

1216-1307.   Brembeley, Brambelheye (T.N.).

1272-1377.   Brambele (P.W.).

   1408.   Brambleley (Ch.).

   1535.   Brameley, Bromeley (V.E.).

   1569.   Bromley (F.F.).

"bramble lea," "pasture or clearing overgrown with brambles" (A.S. bremel, brembel, bræmbel).

Modern outcome due to influence of "broom," M.E. brome, but the words are in any case related.

BROMPTON (brʌmtðn).

    1309.   Bromton (F.F.).
    1481.   Brompton (Escaet).
 ?1526.   Brampton (F.F.).
    1710.   Brompton (Seller).

" broom farm or enclosure."

In the third form above—if it refers to this place—the *a* is due to influence of the related word " bramble."

BRONDESBURY (Kilburn).

    1291.   Brondesbury (T.E.).
    1375.   Bronesbury (F.F.).
    1535.   Brundesbury (V.E.)

The prefix is probably the A.S. personal name *Brand* (Brond), " a sword."   See also p. 99.   Cf. *Bransbury* (Hants), Brandesberee in Dd.

BRUCE CASTLE (Tottenham).

    1312.   manerium de Totenham qð fuit Rob'ti de
               Bruys (Rot. abb).
    1374.   Le Bruses in Totenham (Escaet).
    1487.   Breuses (I.p.m.).
                    etc.

The manor was held by the famous Robert Bruce, who forfeited it, when he fled from the Court of Edward I.

The surname Bruce is Norman from Brieux (formerly Brieus) in France.

BUCKLERSBURY (in the City).

    1284.   Bokerelesberi (A.D.).
    1377.   Bokelersbury (Escaet).
    1535.   Bucklers Bury (V.E.).

" stronghold or manor of Bukerell."

A family of this name held it in 1272 (Harben).   Cf. also Rener' Buckerell in 1235 (Cal. R.C.).   B. is a Norman personal name.

BURTONHALE FARM (Mill Hill).

Burton Hole in Greenwood, Button Hole (*sic !*) in Rocque.
I find no earlier forms, so it may be a modern name.

BURY STREET.

1596.   Bury Street (Norden).

See *Bury* and *Street* (pp. 99 and 105).

Unless Bury was here a man's name.

BUSHEY PARK (Hampton).

c. 1600.   Bushey Park (Mid. Ped.).

Named, according to histories, after *Bushey* (Herts).

See " Place Names of Herts," by the late Prof. Skeat.

CAMBRIDGE HEATH.

1216-1307.   Camprichtesheth, Camprichesheth (H.R.).

1603.   Cambridge Heath (Stowe's).

The prefix is some personal name, perhaps *Cenebriht*
(Coenbeorht).   Cf. *Sawbridgeworth* (Herts) originally *Sæbrihtes
wurþ*.   *nb* would easily be assimilated to *mb*.

CAMDEN TOWN.

Marked in Greenwood's map (1819).   Called after Lord
Camden, who let out the land in 1791 on building leases.

But *Kentish Town* (q.v.) is an old name.

CANONBURY.

1373.   Canonesbury (quoted Lysons).

1374.   Canonsburye (Escaet).

1535.   Canonbury (V.E.).

So named, because a manor held by the prior of the
Augustinian canons of St. Bartholomew at Smithfield.

CANTELOWES (a former manor in St. Pancras).

1190.   Kantelu (P.R.).

1235.   (de) Cantilupo (F.F.).

1235.   Cantelo, Cantalupo (Fees).
1257.   Cantilupe (Fees).
1558-1579.   Cantelowes (L.I., vol. 7).

Other forms quoted in histories are : Cauntelowe, Kaunte-loe, etc.   ? A.F. " can (camp) de lo "—" field of the wolf."

Partially latinized, as was often the case, and anyway an imported name.

CAUSEYWARE HALL (Enfield).
No old forms that I can find.   Perhaps modern.

CHALK FARM.
1596, 1610 }   { (Norden, Speed).
  1710   } Chalcot { (Seller).
1819.   Chalk Farm (Greenwood).

No earlier forms that I can find.   *Chalcot* in Somerset is earlier *Chaldecote*, " cold dwelling."

CHALKHILL (Kingsbury).
1066.   æt Cealchylle (Kble.).
1236.   Chalehull (F.F.) [*e* transcription error for *c* ?]
1240.   Chalkhulle (F.F.).
1483.   Chalkhille (L.I., vol. 16).

Apparently " chalk hill," but the soil here is not such. The name might, however, refer to some peculiar colour of the soil.

CHARING (Cross).
1198.   Cherringe (F.F.).
1232.   Cherring (Ch.).
1243.   Cheryngge (F.F.).
1316.   Charyngge (F.F.).
1369.   By the cross at Cherryng (A.D.).
1397.   Charing Cross (Escaet).

Points to a patronymic of some name * Cærra or * Cearra. The cross dates from the time of Edward I, by whom it was erected as a tribute to Queen Eleanor, whence the popular etymology " chère reine."

But rather doubtful without earlier forms, since *Charing* (Kent) was *Ciornincg* in Bch. No. 293.

CHARLTON.

     1086. Cerdentone (Dd.).
     1232. Cherdinton (F.F.).
     1268. Cherdington (F.F.).
     1316. Cherdyngton (F.A.).
1327-1377 }
    1517 } Chardyngton { (N.I.).
                      (F.F.).
     1539. Charlyngton (F.F.).
     1610. Charlton (Speed).

" farm of the sons of Cerda."

For loss of patronymic, cf. Kenton.

For change of *d* to *l*, cf. Harlington.

Change of *e* to *a* before r + consonant is regular.

CHATTERN HILL (Ashford).

Spelt Chatern in Rocque and Seller.

No earlier forms that I can find, but a good guess, if the name be old, would be " house of Ceatta." (A.S. ærn, " house," " storehouse," " dwelling.")

CHELSEA.

     785. Cealchyðe (Chron.).
     785 }
     789 } Celchyð { (Ind.).
                      (Earle, Kble.).
     799. Cælichyth (Bch., Earle, Ind.).
     825. Cælchyðe (Kble., Thorpe).
     1086. Cerchede, Chelched (Dd.).
     1197. Chelchud' (F.F.).
1272-1377. Chelchehethe (P.W.).
     1291. Chelcheth (T.E.).

1316.   Chelchehuth (F.A.).
1499.   Chelsehithe (F.F.).
1535.   Chelshith (V.E.).
1556.   Chelsyth (F.F.).
1610.   Chelsey (Speed).
1754.   Chelsea (Rocque).

From A.S. *cealc*, " chalk," and *hýð*, " a hithe, wharf, landing place."

As the soil here is not chalk, the name may refer to a " hithe " where chalk or lime was landed for some purpose. *Chelchehithe* is the natural M.E. development, then s > ʃ to facilitate pronunciation and partly through dissimilation.

For loss of final *th* cf. *Stepney* (*infra*). Also *Putney* (Surrey) which was Puttenhuthe, Pottenhethe, Puttenhith in the Surrey Pedes Finium (fourteenth and fifteenth centuries).

CHILDS HILL (Hendon).
1596.   Childes Hill (Norden).

Childe, Chylde (Child) I take to be a man's name. It occurs in the F.F., 1396 and 1485.

CHISWICK (tʃizɪk).

1272-1377	Chesewyk	(P.W.).
1291		(T.E).
1306		(A.D.).
1316		(F.A.).
1428.	Cheswyk (F.A.).	
1558-1603.	Cheesewyke (Proc. Chanc. Eliz.).	
1754.	Chiswick (Rocque).	

" cheese farm or dwelling."   A.S. ćese, ćīese.

The flat meadow lands in the neighbourhood were doubtless early recognized as rich pasture grounds.   [ɪ > ʊ: > e :] cf. *Keswick* (Cumberland).

CLAPTON.

> 1345 ⎱ Clopton ⎰ (L.I., vol. 17).
> 1556 ⎰   ⎱ (F.F.).
> 1581, etc.   Clopton, Clapton (Mem.).
> 1610.   Clapton (Speed).

In a genuine charter, *c.* 880, *Clapham* (Surrey) appears as Cloppaham, and Prof. Skeat thought this must be a genitive plural of a noun * clop, which he compared with Mid. Danish, *klop*, " stub," " stump."

So the meaning may be " farm in the stubby or stumpy ground "—with low bushes and shrubs.

Prof. Mawer, however, considers this solution improbable, so an alternative meaning might be " farm of Cloppa." But Cloppa is only inferred in Searle from the place name Clapham (see above), and it is worth noting that the prefix Clop., Clap. in place names always occurs with *ham* or *ton*, and I think it very unlikely that the numerous Cloptons, Claptons, Claphams in England all come from a personal name.

CLAYHILL (Enfield).

Clay Hill farm marked in Rocque. There is a Clahull (F.F., 1213), but this seems to refer to land near Harefield.

CLERKENWELL (kla : k—).

> *c.* 1100.   juxta fontem clericorum (Dug.).
> 1197.   Clerkenwell (F.F.).
> 1199.   Clerekenewell (P.R.).
> 1200 ⎱   ⎰ (Rot. c.r.).
> 1216-1307 ⎬ Clerkenewell ⎨ (H.R.).
> 1291 ⎰   ⎰ (T.E.).
> 1596.   Clarkenwell (Norden).

The form in Dugdale explains the name ; there were two or three religious houses in the district.

See *clerk* in N.E.D.

CLUTTERHOUSE FARM (Hendon).

    1445.   Clyderhous in Hendon (F.F.).

    1535.   Clitherhouse (V.E.).

    1819.   Clutter House farm (Greenwood).

Named after a family Cliderhou—cf. Robert de Cliderhou in F.F., 1311. This surname comes from Cliderhou, Clitherou (Lancs)—now *Clitheroe*.

The modern outcome is due to folk-etymology.

COCKFOSTERS (Enfield).

    1632.   Cock ffosters (E. Cass' "East Barnet").

    1819.   Cock Forsters (Greenwood).

G. L. states that *cock* may = old French bicoque, "a little hut or hovel," but this is doubtful.

Might not *cock* = "chief" in this instance and the meaning be "(dwelling) of the chief forester"?

Cockfosters is a hamlet on the outskirts of Enfield Chase.

COLDHARBOUR FARM (Hayes).

Prof. Skeat explained this name as meaning a harbour or refuge where one could get shelter but no food or fire.

N.E.D. says: "Cold Harbour, a place of shelter from the weather for wayfarers, constructed by the wayside."

There are many places of this name in England.

COLHAM.

    831.   Colanhomm (Ind., Kble.).

    1086 } Coleham { (Dd.).
    1198 }   { (F.F.).

    1210.   Colnham (R.E.).

    1291.   Coleham (T.E.).

    1331.   Colham (Ch.).

    1434.   Colnham (Ind.).

This might mean "enclosure of Cola," and the river Colne a "back formation" from it.

2

Prof. Mawer, however, considers the Colne to be a genuine river name, so the meaning will be "enclosure by the river Colne."

There is no appreciable bend in the Colne here to justify the interpretation "bend"—see p. 103.

The modern Colham is some distance from the river.

COLNE RIVER (koun).

Probably of Celtic origin. Gloucestershire *Colne* was originally *Cunngl, Cunelga*, etc., but the oldest forms of the Hertfordshire *Colne* are Colen and Colne (893 Chron.), cf. also *colenéa* in Kble. = Colney (Herts).

The Colne is really a Herts river, though it forms the western boundary of Middlesex in the lower part of its course.

COLNEY FARM (Harefield).

1561.   Colney (F.F.).

Assuming that the river Colne is an old name, Colney must be so called from close proximity to it.   Otherwise it might = "island of Cola," *Colan eꝫ.

COLNEY HATCH.

1507.   Colne Hatch (quoted Lysons).
1596, 1610.   Cony Hatch (Norden, Speed).
1710.   Coanie Hatch (Seller).
1754.   Colney Hatch (Rocque).

Since this place is nowhere near the river Colne, it cannot be associated with the preceding names.

The sense here must be either "island of Cola," or else "rabbit"—M.E., coni, conni.

Hatch refers to a side gate of Enfield Chase.   See p. 103.

* COPENHAGEN FIELDS (Islington).

Coopen Hagen in Camden, Copenhagen in Rocque. Named after an inn kept by a Dane, *temp.* James I, according to histories. Marked on maps down to *c.* 1850, when the cattle-market was built on the site.

The name remains in the Copenhagen Tunnel on the G.N.R. main line.

COPTHALL FARM (Ickenham).
          1532.   Coppydhall (F.F.).
hall may stand for *hale.*   (See p. 102.)

With the prefix we may compare Copdock (Suffolk) and Copthorne (Surrey) where the sense is " copped," i.e. pollarded.

Its sense here is not so obvious, but cf. Copthall in Essex, which was Coppedehalle in the thirteenth century.

CORNHILL (in the City).
     c. 1130.   Cornhilla (quoted Harben).
          1183.   Cornhill (P.R.)
          1202.   Cornhill, Cornhull (Rot. Canc.).
     1216-1307.   Cornhulle, Cornhelle, Cornhille (H.R.).

Stow says that a corn market had been held here " time out of mind."

CORNHILL (Greenford).
          1313.   Cornhull (Ch.).

Here the meaning may be, " hill where corn was grown."

COWHOUSE FARM (Childs Hill).
          1398.   Cowhous (Ch.).

COWLEY.
     ‡ 959.   Cofenlea (Kble., Thorpe).
        998.   Cofanlea (Thorpe).
       1086.   Covelei (Dd.).
       1204.   Coueleg (F.F.).
       1272.   Covele *(Escaet).*
       1316.   Couele (F.A.).

1428.   Cowle (F.A.).

1535.   Couley, Cowley (V.E.).

" pasture or clearing of Cūfa."

Loss of medial " v " (cf. Harlesden), and usual development of A.S. ū.

COWLEY PEACHEY.

1252.- Grant to Bartholemew Pecche . . . lands in Coueleg and Ikenham, Co. Middlesex (Ch.).

" Peach " is still in use as a surname.

CRANFORD.

1086.   Cranforde (Dd.).

1210.   Craunforde (R.E.).

1231 } Cranford { (F.F.).
1291 }   { (T.E.).

1301.   Craunford (Pat.).

1428.   Craneford (F.A.).

" crane ford," the meaning being either " ford frequented by cranes" or " ford over which a crane could wade "—and hence a means of judging its depth.

The river *Crane* I take to be a back formation.

CRICKLEWOOD (Hendon).

So marked in Seller (1710).   Krickle Wood in Rocque (1754).   I cannot find earlier forms, but Johnston quotes a " Crekyll Woddes " (1525) and " Crekle Woods " (1553), though without references.

Perhaps originally " crinkle wood "—cf. Dutch *krinkel*, " twist," " turn," and *crickle* in N.E.D. = " a tangle."

CRIPPLEGATE (a City gate).

c. 1000.   Cripelesgate (quoted Harben).

1068.   Crepelesgate (quoted Harben).

1204.   Cripelgate (F.F.).   .

1216-1307.   Crepelgate, Cripelgate, Cruppelgate (H.R.).
   1315.   Crypelgate (F.F.), etc.
The forms in Harben point to a "gate of Cripel (Crypel),"
but the later forms answer to a "cripple gate," i.e. gate where
cripples lay.
This latter is the most likely solution, beggars no doubt
swarming at the city gates.
Moreover there is no evidence that "Crypel" was used as
a personal name in A.S.

CROUCH END (Hornsey).
   1400.   Geoffrey atte Crouche . . . of Harengey (A.D.).
   1466.   Crouchend (A.D.).
   1481.   Crowchende (A.D.).
   1610.   Cruch Ende (Speed).
M.E. cruche, crouche.   A.S. crúc, "a cross," ultimately
from the Latin crux, cruc-.
Cf. the surname *Crouch* and the *Crutched Friars* in the
"City."   *End* in the sense of "boundary," "limit."

CUBITT TOWN (Isle of Dogs).
Modern.   Named after William Cubitt (c. 1850) to whom
the building of the church and most of the houses round about
is due (Besant).

CUCKOO FARM (Ruislip).
Marked in Greenwood (1819).   Probably a nickname.

DALSTON (Hackney) [dɔːlstən].
   1388.   Dorleston (F.F.).
1581, etc.   Dorleston, Darleston, Darlston (Mem.).
   1754.   Dalston (Rocque).
Probably "farm of Deórlaf," A.S. * Deórlafes tún.   Cf.
Darleston (Warwickshire).
The modern spelling means nothing.   The name would be
pronounced the same (in London) were it spelled * Dorleston,

DANCERSHILL (Mimms).

So spelt in Norden (1596).   Dancer was probably a man's name.   It is still in use as a surname.

DAWLEY (Hayes).

        1086.   Dallega (Dd.).
    c. 1200.   Dallee (Rot. c.r.).
        1210.   Dalle (R.E.).
        1312.   Dalley (F.F.).
        1710.   Doyley (Seller).
        1754.   Dawley (Rocque).

Prefix probably A.S. *dāl,* "portion," "allotment," "division," "dole"; perhaps referring to land parcelled out to various owners.

* DERNFORD (Tottenham).

        1412.   Derneford (F.F.).

Probably A.S. * se dyrna (dierna), ford = "the secret or hidden ford," cf. *Durnford* (Wilts).

DOLLIS HILL (Hendon).

Spelt Dolleys (Hill) in Greenwood, Dollys in Rocque, Dallis in Seller, Daleson in Norden.

Called after some man Dolley, Dalley or Dollison.   This surname may be derived from *Dawley* (above).

DOWGATE (a City gate).

        1067⎫   ⎛(quoted Harben).
        1150⎬ Duuegate ⎨   (do.).
        1174⎭   ⎝   (do.).
    1216-1307.   Douegate, Dowgate (H.R.).
        1428.   Douegate (F.A).
        1538.   Dowgate (F.F.).

There is a Duuua (Duwa) in Searle but it is "nomen mulieris," so I prefer to assume a hypothetical Dūfa (cf. Cowley).

Female names were rare as first elements in place names.

Down Barns (Northolt).

1272-1377.   La Doune (P.W.).
1355.   la Doune (Ind.).
1361.   Doune (F.F.).
1535.   Downebarnes (V.E.).

"at the down or hill."   M.E. dun(e), doun(e).   A.S. dūn.
The "barnes" is a late addition.

The 1-inch ordnance map shows a small hill here.

Drayton, West Drayton.

939.   Drægtun (Bch.).
‡ 989.   Draitune (Kble.).
1086.   Draitone (Dd.).
1291.   Drayton (T.E.).
1316.   Dreyton (F.A.).
1485.   West Drayton (Escaet).

Prof. Skeat compared this prefix to provincial English *dray*, "a squirrel's nest" (see E.D.D.) and assumed an A.S. *(ge) dræg(e), "a retreat," "nook."

There are many places with this prefix in England, and in almost every case the suffix is -*cott* or -*ton*.

The meaning is generally taken to be "hidden homestead or farm," "isolated dwelling."

Ealing.

1165.   Illing (Mag. Rot.).
1244, 1246.   Gilling' (F.F.).
1272-1377.   Gillyng (P.W.).
1316.   Yilling (F.A.).
1327-1377.   Yellynge (N.I.).
1399.   Zyllyng (L.I., vol. 5).
1428.   Zylling (F.A.).
1521.   Elyng (F.F.).
1535.   Yelling (V.E.)
1622.   Ealing al. Yealing (Ind.).

"Place of the Gillingas."   Searle has a Gillus and Gillo.

The *z* in the above forms is of course the M.E. symbol ȝ, which indicated a sound (j), or something similar. The initial (j) sound is here lost before the long vowel following. It is retained in *Yelling* (Hunts).

EARLS COURT (Kensington).

  1558-1579.   Earls Court (L.I., vol. 7).
  1593, 1609.   Earl's Court in Kensington (L.I., vol. 6).
    1623.   Earles Court (Mid. Ped.).

So called, because the court house of the de Veres, Earls of Oxford, stood here.   They had held the manor of Kensington since the Conquest.   (See M'sex. Dd.)

EASTCOTE.

    1296.   Estcote (S.S., vol. 2).
  1596, 1710.   Ascot (Norden ; Seller).
    1819.   Eastcote (Greenwood).

"east dwelling or house," i.e. east of Ruislip.

The modern form is partly artificial ; the forms in Norden and Seller show the normal development.   In the F.F. I find also a *Northcote* (1250), *Suthcote* (1342, 1402) and *Westcote* (1310), but these places seem to be no longer represented on the modern ordnance map.

EBURY, "EYE."

    1086.   Eia (Dd.).
    1206.   Eya (F.F.).
    1316 ⎫   ⎧ (F.A.)
    1383 ⎬   Eye ⎨ (Escaet).
    1406 ⎭   ⎩ (A.D.).
    1300.   Euberye (Escaet).
    1324.   Eyghebury (I.p.m.).
  1308, 1325.   Eyebury (L I., vol. 5).
    1535.   Eybery, Eybury, Ebery (V.E.).

Eia, Eyai s merely a latinized form of A.S. ēȝ, iēȝ, "island."
—See p. 101.

Bury is a later addition.   See p. 99.

The name remains in Ebury Square and Street (West-minster).

EDGEWARE.

972.	Ægces wer (Bch.).
1169, etc.	Eggeswere (P.R.).
1198 } 1226 }	Egeswere { (F.F.). { (Ind.).
1272-1377.	Eggeswere (P.W.).
1331.	Eggewere (Ch.).
1426.	Eggeware (Escaet).
1541.	Edgeware (F.F.).

Suffix is A.S. *wer,* "weir," "dam," "fishing pool."

Prefix is a personal name Ecg (Ecge, Æcge).

The A.S. *ecg,* "sword"—literally "edge"—was used as a first element in numerous personal names, and *Ecga* (whence the surname "Edge") was used as a shortened or "pet" form of one of these names.   The strong form Ecg, Ecge is not in Searle, but was probably in use also.

EDMONTON.

1086.	Adelmetone (Dd.).
1182.	Ædelmeton (P.R.).
ante 1200.	Eadelmeton (Ind.).
1210.	Edelmintone (R.E.).
1214 } 1216-1307 }	Edelmeston { (Rot. L.C.). { (T.N.).
1235.	Edelmestun (Fees.).
1291 } 1316 }	Edelmeton { (T.E.). { (F.A.).
1369.	Edmenton (A.D.).
1397.	Edmunton (Escaet).

1397. Edelmynton (F.F.).
1422. Edelmyngton (F.F.).
1424. Edmyngton (F.F.).
1464. Edelmeton *alias* Edmonton (Escaet.).
1492. Edmondton (F.F.).
1535. Edelmeton, Edmundton, Edmonton (V.E.).

There are two types (1) *Eadhelmes tún—as in Rot. L.C., T.N., and Fees.   (2) *Eadhelminga tún, a patronymic.

The modern outcome is due to Type (2), the development being similar to that of *Admington* (Gloucester).

In the case of Edmonton, however, the prefix was associated with the Christian name Edmund, whence the modern form.

The *el* appears to have been lost as early as 1369.

ELSTREE (really in Herts, but part of the town is shown in the ordnance map to be in Middlesex).

785. fram Tiðulfes tréow (Kble.).
12th cent. Tidulvestre (quoted V.C.H., Herts).
13th cent. Tydolvestre   (do.).
c. 1200. Thidolvestre (Rot. c.r.).
c. 1250. Tydulvestre, Idulvestre (Dug.).
1274⎫
1275⎭ Idulvestre ⎰(A.D.).
            ⎱(F.F.).
1272-1377. Idolvestre (P.W.).
1377⎫
1408⎭ Idelstre ⎰(A.D.).
          ⎱(F.F.).
1550. Ilestre (F.F.).
1610. Elstre (Speed).

"at the tree of Tidwulf"—probably marking some boundary. The modern outcome shows a rather violent contraction, but there are many similar cases in England, *Golcar* (Yorks), *Hersham* (Surrey), etc.

Loss of initial *t* is due to preposition *at* (see *Ickenham*). For loss of *v* cf. *Harlesden*.   Finally *dl* < *ll* by assimilation.

ELTHORNE (name of a "Hundred").

     1086.   Heletorne, Helethorne (Dd.).
     1169.   Ellethorn (P.R.).
     1176.   Ellesthorn (P.R.).
     1183.   Helethorn (Ind.).
 1216-1307.   Ellethorn (H.R.).
     1428.   Elethorn (F.A.).

"at the thorn (tree) of Ælla."   See p. 106.

Ælla is a known A.S. name, borne by the conqueror of Sussex for example.

The initial *h* is meaningless, and betrays a Norman scribe.

ENFIELD.

     1086.   Enefelde (Dd.).
     1205.   Ainefeld (Rot. L.C.).
     1210.   Enefeude (R.E.).
 1216-1307.   Enesfeud (T.N.).
     1219 ⎫ Enefeld ⎰ (F.F.).
     1248 ⎭   ⎱ (Ch.).
     1464.   Enfeld (F.F.).
     1535.   Endefeild (V.E.).
     1638.   Endfeild (Ind.).

A.S. * Ænan feld, "clear open space of Æna." See p. 101. The *d* in the late forms is excrescent, due, perhaps, to the influence of the word "end."

ENFIELD CHASE.

     1326.   park and chace of . . . Enefeld (Close).
     1530.   Endefeld Chace (L.P.H.).

Chase is old French, *chace*, "hunting ground," "tract of unenclosed land for breeding and hunting wild animals," etc.

N.E.D. gives first appearance of the word in English as 1297.

The following local names on the 1-inch ordnance map were all connected formerly with E. Chase :—

Cattlegate. Chase Farm. Chase Cottage. Chase Side. East, North, South, West Lodge, Oak Lodge. Gannic Corner (Gannoc, a man's name), *Sanders Corner.*

Also *Cockfosters, Potters Bar,* and *Southgate* (q.v.).

FALLOW CORNER (Finchley).

Marked in Speed's map (1610).

Here probably in the sense of "fallow land," i.e. "land lying untilled and unsown periodically."

FARRINGDON (a City ward).

   1281. Farindon (A.D.).
   1300. Farndon (Cor.).
   1329. Farendon (Escaet).
   1383. Faryngdon (A.D.).
   1428. Farndon (F.A.).
       etc.

According to Harben named after a William de Farndon in 1280, so not an original Middlesex name.

Farndon may = "fern down," or contain a patronymic; it depends on which place in England this particular man came from.

FELTHAM.

   ‡969. Feltham (Bch., Kble., Thorpe).
   1086. Felteham (Dd.).
   1213⎫   ⎧(F.F.).
   1228⎬ Feltham ⎨(Ch.).
   1316⎭   ⎩(F.A.).

Subsequent forms all similar.

N.E.D. gives some M.E. forms of *field* (feld) "felt," but the Dd. form is against this derivation.

There is no name * Felta in Searle, and the only possible derivation seems to be A.S. *felt,* "felt."

If the original suffix was "hamm" the epithet might have referred to the smooth dead level grassy country here.

FENCHURCH.

    c. 1170.   Fenchirche (quoted Harben).

    1292.   Fanchirche (A.D.).

    1300.   Fencherche (I.p.m).

    1535.   Fanchurche (V.E.).

                etc.

"church in the fen or marshy spot."

The Langbourn stream ran near by.

FIELDEND FARM (near Eastcote).

    Field End in Rocque.   Meaning obvious.

FINCHLEY.

    1243.   Fynchesl' (F.F.).

    1272-1377.   Fynchesleye (P.W.).

    1291.   Finchisle (T.E.).

    1316.   Fynchesle (F.A.).

    1428.   Fyncheley (F.A.).

"pasture or clearing of * Finc." A.S. *finc*, "finch," is not recorded as a personal name, but must have been so used, as the genitival *s* shows [ʃðsl—ʃsl—ʃl].

Finch is now used as a surname.

FINSBURY.

    1216-1307.   Finesbur' (H.R.).

    1272.   Fynesbyr (F.F.).

    1316.   Fynesbury (F.A.).

    1397.   Vynesbury (Escaet).

    1535.   Fynnesbury, Fenysbury (V.E.).

The prefix is a personal name Fin or Finn. As an example of the latter, Searle notes a king of the North Frisians. For second element see p. 99.

FLEET (river).

    1199.   Flete (Cal. Rot. Ch.).

    1202.   Fliete (Rot. Canc.).

1277.   Flete (Escaet).
1280.   Flete strete (I.M.).

A.S. *flēot*, " channel," " stream," " running water," the name being perhaps applied to the short navigable part of the river.   Cf. *Byfleet* (Surrey), " Bifleote " in Kble., *anno* 1062.

FORTY HILL (Enfield).

So spelt in Rocque, who also has a *Forty Green* near Finchley, now *Fortis Green*.
Possibly " four tree hill."   Cf. *feower treowe hyl* in Kble.

FRITH MANOR (Hendon).
1294.   Fryth (F.F.).
1535.   Fryth in Hendon (V.E.).
1571.   Frith al. Newhall (Ind.).

M E. *frith* = " a deer park," " plantation," " preserve," " wood " > A.S. *friðu*, " peace."   See N.E.D. sub *frith*.

FROGMORE FARM and FROGMORE GREEN (Hayes).

No forms earlier than the eighteenth century that I can find.   Probably to be interpreted literally.

FROGNAL (Hampstead).
1542.   Frogenhall (F.F.).

Possibly " frog nook or retreat."   See *Hale*, p. 102   Or *Frocga* may have been used as a personal name, though it is not in Searle.

FULHAM.
879, 881.   on, æt, Fullanhamme (Chron.).
1052.   Fullenham (Kble.).
1086.   Fuleham (Dd.).
1172.   Fulehā (P.R.).
1197.   Folehā (P.R.).
1232.   Foleham (F.F.).
1312.   Folleham (S.S., vol. 33).

1326.   Fulleham (F.F.).

1428.   Fulham (F.A.).

Ful- as a prefix to English place names sometimes goes back to A.S. fŭl, " foul," " dirty," but the forms above show that in this case the prefix must be A.S. *ful,* " full."

The second element is A.S. *hamm* (see p. 103) and since Fulham is situated in a large bend of the Thames the meaning may be " at the full—crowded, overstocked?—bend or ' ham '."

The land is dead level, and was doubtless entirely cultivated from early times.

GOLDERS GREEN (Hendon).

1695.   Goulders Green (Camden).

Goulder or Golder was a man's name. Cf. also GOULDS GREEN (Hayes), so marked in Rocque (1754).

GORE (name of a Hundred).

1086.   Gara, Gare (Dd.).

1169.   Gar (P.R.).

1216-1307 }
1428 }   Gore { (H.R.).
               { (F.A.).

1610.   Goare (Speed).

A.S. *gára,* " corner of land," " triangular shaped piece of land," from *gár,* " a spear."

We have also *Kensington Gore,* where stood *Gore House,* now demolished.

GOSPEL OAK (Hampstead).

Marked in Greenwood (1819). Rocque has another Gospel Oak near Ealing.

The name refers to places where an open-air preacher held forth in former times during Rogation week.

GOSWELL (in the City).

    No date.   Godewelle (quoted Harben).

    1197. Godewell (F.F.).

    1219 $\left.\right\}$ Gosewell $\left\{\right.$ (Fees).
    1216-1307 (T.N.).

    1370. Goswell (Escaet).

Looks like an A.S. *Gōdan wielle, "well of Gōda," i.e. "Good," the change of *d* to *s* being due perhaps to association with "goose."

The name remains in the Goswell Road.

GRACECHURCH (in the City).

    1198.   Garschirch (P.R.).

    1200.   Garscherch (A.D.).

    1291.   Grascherche, Grescherch (T.E.).

    1298.   Greschirche (Ind.).

    1355.   Grasecherche (Ind.).

    1390.   Gracechurche (Escaet).

Prefix probably A.S. græs, gærs. M.E. gras, gres, gars, gers, "grass"—referring to a church surrounded by grass. (G. was always in the City of London, so the epithet might refer to a City church surrounded by lawns.)   Prof. Mawer thinks this solution unlikely, but I can suggest no other.

Garston (Surrey) was Garston, Gerston, Greston in the Surrey fines (Surrey Arch. Soc. Add., vol. I).

GREENFORD.

    845.   et [= æt] grenan forda (Bch.).

    ‡ 1066 $\left.\right\}$ (Ind., Kble., Thorpe).
    1086 Greneford (Dd.).
    1210 (R.E.).
    1291 (T.E.).

    1343. Grenford (I.p.m.).

"At the green ford," perhaps because the vegetation here was unusually luxuriant—as opposed to some other.

GREENHILL (Harrow).

    1479.   Grenehill (F.F.).

    1695.   Green Hill (Camden).

GREEN LANES (Hornsey).

Marked in seventeenth to nineteenth century maps. Formerly descriptive.

GREEN STREET (Enfield).

    1596.   Gren strete (Norden).

street may have sense of "scattered hamlet." See p. 105.

GUNNERSBURY.

  1348, 1390.   Gunnyldesbury (F.F.).

  1364, 1373.   Gonyldesbury (Close).

      1377.   Gunnyldesbery (Escaet).

      1380.   Gonyldesbury (Ind.).

      1486.   Gonelsbury (Escaet).

      1531.   Gonelbury otherwise Goneldisbury (F.F.).

      1610.   Gunnersbury (Speed).

Prefix is a personal name Gunhild—later Gunnild, Gunilda. This is a feminine name and the *s* may be explained by the fact that personal names as first elements of place names were almost always masculine.

But it is very doubtful if the place name is as old as the Norman Conquest, though Histories like to associate it with Gunhild, niece of King " Canute."

rs $>$ ls by interchange of liquids.   ls $\geqslant$ lds by simplification of consonant group.

GUTTERIDGE WOOD (S.E. of Ickenham).

Spelt *Grutedge* in Rocque (1754).   No earlier forms that I can find, but cf. *Scrattage* (*infra*), the suffix being evidently *edge* in both cases.

HACKNEY.
>   1231. Hakney (F.F.).
>   1216-1307⎫   ⎧(T.N.).
>   1272-1377⎬ Hakeneye ⎨(P.W.).
>   1316   ⎭   ⎩(F.A.).
>   1535. Hackeney, Hackney, (V.E.).

The first element is a personal name *Haca.* For the second element, see p. 101.

Cf. *Hackbridge* (Surrey), " Hakebrug " in thirteenth century (Index).

HACKNEY WICK.
>   1242. la Wyke (F.F.).
>   1549. Wyke (F.F.).
>   1754. Wick (Rocque).

A.S. *wic,* " dwelling," " house," " abode."   See p. 107.

HADLEY.
>   1216-1307⎫   ⎧(T.N.).
>   1272-1377⎭ Hadleye ⎨(P.W.).
>   1291. Hadle, Hedle (T.E.).
>   1348. Haddeleye (F.F.).
>   1349, 1365. Hadele (F.F.).
>   1394. Hadle (F.F.).
>   1483. Hadley Monachorum (F.F.).
>   1489. Monken Hadley (F.F.).
>   1535. Hedlegh (V.E.).

The first element is a personal name Head(d)a.   For the second element see p. 104.

The words Monken, Monachorum show that the place was at one time monastic property.

HAGGERSTON.
>   1086. Hergotestane (Dd.).
>   1216-1307. Hargoldestone, Hargodelston (H.R.).

1303.   Hargodeston (F.F.).
c. 1470.   Argeston (L.I., vol. 16).
1549.   Argarston (F.F.).
1554.   Hargolston (F.F.).
1561.   Agerston (F.F.).

"at the stone of Heregod or * Heregold."
rs > ls > lds.   Cf. *Gunnersbury*.

HALE (Edgeware).
1216-1307.   la Hale (H.R.)
1327-1377.   The Hale (N.I.).
1525.   Hale (F.F.).
1710.   The Hale (Seller).

Old Mercian *halh*, (dative "hale"). (A.S. healb, heale). A word of frequent occurrence in charters and apparently meaning "a nook," "corner," "retreat."

The word occurs as a suffix in many Middlesex names, in the disguised forms, -ale, -ell, -al, -hall, -holt, etc.

HALIWELL (Shoreditch).
1235.   Haliwell (Ch.).
1282.   Haliwelle (F.F.).
1377.   Haliwell (Dug.).
1428 ⎫
1440 ⎭   Halywell ⎰ (F.A.).
                   ⎱ (F.F.).

"holy well or spring."

* HALIWICK (Barnet).
1235.   Hallewyc (F.F.).
1376 ⎫
1402 ⎭   Halewyk ⎰ (Close).
                  ⎱ (Escaet).
1596.   Hollick (Norden).

"holy spot or dwelling."

3 *

HALLIFORD.

      962.   to halgan forda (Earle, p. 293).

    ‡ 969⎤   ⎧(Bch., Kble., Thorpe).
    1202⎬ Halgeforde⎨(Rot. Canc.).
    1208⎦   ⎩(F.F.).

    1252. Halheford (F.F.).

    1264. Halegheford, Halegeford (F.F.).

    1279. Haleweford (F.F.).

1272-1377. Halgford (P.W.).

    1285. Halweford (Escaet).

    1316. Halgheford (F.A.).

    1349. Netherhalford (F.F.).

    1421. Uphalleford (F.F.).

    1819. Halliford (Greenwood).

Not "holy ford," but rather "ford of the saint or holy person." See the old forms of "holy" and "hallow" in the N.E.D.

HAMMERSMITH.

    1312.   Hameresmythe, Hameresmithe (S.S., vol. 33).

1313, 1380. Hamersmyth (F.F.).

    1386.   Hamersmytthe (F.F.).

    1642.   Hamersmith (Ind.).

Suffix must be A.S. (ge)mýðe, "mouth of river," "junction of two rivers." Cf. the *Mythe* (Glos.).

Old maps mark a small stream flowing into the Thames here. Or possibly the great bend in the river at this point gave rise to a fanciful or humorous suggestion of two rivers meeting.

Prefix is a personal name, probably Heahmær (Hæmar).

There is a "Hammersbach" in Germany.

HAMMOND'S FARM (Staines).

    1544. Hamondes (F.F.).

probably named after Robert Hamond (F.F., 1534).

The surname Ham(m)ond is Norman Hamon (with excrescent *d*) of Teutonic origin cognate with the A.S. name Haganmund (Weekley).

HAMPSTEAD.

> 978. Hamstede (Bch.).
> 986. Ham stede (Ind.).
> 998. Hamstede (Th.).
> 1066. Heamstede (Ind., Kble., Thorpe).
> 1086. Hamestede (Dd.).
> 1232 ⎫
> 1242 ⎬ Hamsted ⎰ (F.F.). (Ch.). (T.E.).
> 1291 ⎭
> 1316. Hampstede (F.A.).

A.S. hám stede, " home stead or place," assuming that the 986 Index form is genuine.

HAMPTON.

> 781. Homtune (quoted in Johnston).
> 1086. Hamntone (Dd.).
> 1200. Hamton (Rot. c.r.).
> 1237. Hampton (F.F.).
>   etc.

A.S. hamm tún, i.e. " enclosure in a bend of the River " (Thames).

Dd. *mn* is difficult to explain unless an error for *mm*.

HAMPTON WICK.

> 1263. Hamptone la Wyke (F.F.).
> 1289. Hampton a la Wyke (F.F.).
> 1428. Wyke (Ind.).
>   Cf. Hackney Wick.

HANGERHILL (Ealing).

    1610.   Hanger Woode (Speed).

    1710.   Hanger Hill (Seller).

A.S. *hangra*, " wood situated on a hill slope," " hanging wood."

HANWELL.

    ‡ 959.   Hanewelle (Thorpe).

    ‡ 998.   Hanawella (Thorpe).

    1066.   Hanawelle (Index).

    1086.   Hanewelle (Dd.).

    1150 }
    1291 } Hanewell { (Ind.).
    { (T.E.).

    1428.   Hanwell (F.A.).

A.S. * Hanan welle, " well or spring of Hana."

In Kble., No. 331, we actually have " ærest on hanan welle, siððan on hanan wurðe," though these do not, I think, refer to the Middlesex places.

HANWORTH.

    1086.   Haneworde (Dd.).

    1210.   Hanewrth (R.E.).

    1216-1307 }
    1272-1377 } Haneworth { (T.N.).
    { (P.W.).

    1428.   Hanworth (F.A.).

" farm or enclosure of Hana."   See p. 107 and cf. preceding. The literal meaning of *hana* is " cock."

HAREFIELD.

    1086.   Herefelle (Dd.).

    1176.   Herrefeld (P.R.).

    1206.   Herefeld (F.F.).

    1213.   Herrefeld (F.F.).

    1219.   Heresfeld (Excerpta).

1216-1307.   Herefeld, Harefeld (T.N.).

1327. Herefeld (F.F.).
1350. Herfeld (F.F.).
1393. Harfeld (Escaet).

The prefix looks like A.S. *here*, "army," the sense being perhaps "open space where an army was encamped." The name may date from some period during the Danish Invasions. Cf. *Hereford*.

er + cons. < ar + cons. is regular, cf. *Clerkenwell*.

HARLESDEN.

1086. Herulvestune (Dd.).
1191. Herlesdon (T.E.).
1327. Herleston (F.F.).
1327-1377. Herlaston (N.I.).
1535. Harleston (V.E.).
1606. Harlesden (Ind.).

"farm or enclosure of Herulf (Herewulf)." Cf. *Harleston*, near Bungay (Suffolk).

For dropping of *v* cf. Elstree. ar > er as preceding.

HARLINGTON.

825 }
969 } hygereding tun { (Kble.).
                      { (Bch.).
1086. Herdintone (Dd.).
1235. Herdinton (F.F.).
1291. Herdyngton (T.E.).
1475. Hardlyngton (F.F.).
1535. Hardington, Harlington (V.E.).
1610. Harlington (Speed).

"farm of the sons of Hygered."

Prof. Mawer thinks Dd. *Herd* for earlier *hygered*, possible. There must have been intermediate forms *hiered*, *hierd*. For change of *d* to *l* (through *dl* ?) cf. *Charlton*.

HARMONDSWORTH.

    1086. Hermodesworde (Dd.).

    1248} Hermodesworth {(S.S., vol. 2).
    1295}   {(F.F.).

    1316} Hermondesworth {(F.A.).
    1391}   {(Pat.).

    1428. Harmansworth (F.A.).

    15th century. Harmsworth (L.I., vol. 16).

    1552} Harmesworth {(F.F.).
    1596}   {(Norden).

    1610. Hamsworth (Speed).

    1754. Harmondsworth (Rocque).

"farm or holding of Heremōd."   See p. 107.

Later *n* inserted as in the word *messenger* (q.v. in N.E.D.). The spelling "Harmondsworth" is a mere artificial restoration. The natural outcome should be *Harmsworth, which is attested by some of the above forms and by the well-known surname. The place was still so pronounced by the "natives" at the beginning of last century (G.L.), but the written word is becoming all powerful nowadays.

The Rev. W. B. Sealey, vicar of Harmondsworth, who has kindly made inquiries, informs me that the place is still pronounced [ha:mzwð:θ, ha·mzðθ] by "the older people" of the neighbourhood, but that the "younger generations" tend to "pronounce as written."

HARRINGAY.

   See under *Hornsey* (*infra*).

   The two words are the same, just as are "chance" and "cadence."

HARROW.

    767. Gumeninga hergae (Bch., Kble.).

    825. æt Hearge (Bch., Ind., Thorpe).

1086.   Herges (Dd.).
1232.   Hereghes (Ch.).
1235.   Herghes (F.F.).
1216-1307. Harrewe (H.R.).
1243.   Hergh' (F.F.).
1316⎫
1327-1377⎭ Harwe ⎧(F.A.).
          ⎩(N.I.).
1368.   Harogh' (F.F.).
1479.   Harowe atte hill (F.F.).
1535.   Harrowe on the hill (V.E.).

A.S. *hearh, hearg*—dative *hearge* = "a heathen temple or place of worship." Such places were often on hill-tops, but their traces are few, since the English usually destroyed them on their conversion to Christianity. The * Gumeningas were probably a tribe who held the place, or possibly even the temple priests.

Cf. *Peperharow* (Surrey), Pipareherge (Dd.), Pyperhargh (T.E.), which undoubtedly contains the same word.

The phonetic development of the name is exactly similar to the word "marrow" (q.v. in N.E.D.), and the *s* in some of the above forms is "simply a sign of the plural. The word might well so be used" (Prof. Mawer).

HARROW WEALD.

1303.   (Land in) Waldis in the parish of Harwes (A.D.).
1382⎫
1550⎭ Welde ⎧(A.D.).
        ⎩(F.F.).
1553.   Harrow Weelde (F.F.).

A.S. weald, wald = "wood," "wooded country," which took in M.E. the sense of "waste land," "wild open country."

The normal outcome of A.S. *wald* is "wold," but there appears to have been a related form *wæld*, whence M.E. weld, weeld, weald.

HATCH END.

> 1393. . . . atte Hacche of Harowe (F.F.).
> 1475. Hacheend (F.F.).
> 1710. Hatch End (Seller).

See both elements on pp. 101, 103.

HATTON.

> 1086. Hatone, Hattone (Dd.).
> 1210. Hattone (R.E.).
> 1213)
> 1233} Hatton {(F.F.).
>   {(F.F.).
> 1373. Haddon (Escaet).
> 1403. Haddon *juxta* Hundeslowe (Escaet).
> 1554. Hatton (F.F.).

Probably A.S. * hæð tún, "farm on the heath." [tt > tht.]
This suits the situation of the place. Cf. *Hatfield* (Herts).

HAVERSTOCK HILL (Hamstead).

Marked in Rocque. H. was the name of a house.

Probably an imported name, since *stock* is not a Middlesex suffix, and *haver* = " oats," is a north country word.

HAYES.

> 793. linganhese, lingahæse (Bch.).
> 831. hæse (Bch.).
> 831. hyse (Kble, Thorpe).
> 1086. Hesa (Dd.).
> 1232. Hese (Ch.).
> 1248. Haes (S.S., vol. 2).
> 1291)
> 1316} Hese {(T.E.).
>   {(F.A.).
> 1498. Heys (F.F.).
> 1535. Hayes (V.E.).

1541, 1557, 1561. Hees, Heese (F.F.).

The supplement to Bosworth's A.S. dictionary gives:

"hese, hẏse, haese, hoese," "brushwood," "land with bushes and brushwood," quoting some examples from charters.

Kemble says: "hoese, hyse, apparently brushwood, and as far as I have observed, always pasture for swine, cf. O.N. heisi, 'poor thin grass'."

Hayes in Kent has similar old forms, and probably in many cases the prefix Has- Hes- in place names has this meaning.

I cannot explain the *linga, lingan.* *Ling* = " heather" is of Norse origin.

HEADSTONE (Pinner).

  1398. Heggeton (Escaet).
  1526. Hegestone (L.I., vol. 34).
  1754. Hedston (Rocque).

Perhaps A.S. *hecg tún, "farm enclosed by a hedge."

"Hedge stone" is a less likely meaning, and anyway the modern outcome could be explained [dʒ—dz], the medial *e* in the 1526 form being of no importance, as it was by then silent in pronunciation at the end of a word or syllable.

In the Rev. W. D. Bushell's "Church Life on Harrow Hill," I note the following forms quoted "de la Hegge," c. 1390, Heggedon, 1382, Heggeston, 1545; so that the *s* does not seem to be original.

HEATHROW.

  ?1551. Heth (F.F.).
  1553. Hitherowe (F.F.).
  1710. Hetherow (Seller).
  1754. Heath Row (Rocque).

Referring to a row of houses or small hamlet on the heath.

The *i* in the 1553 form may be a transcription error, but in any case the prefix could not be "hithe" as the place is not near any stream or river.

Hendon.

   972. [oþ] heandunes gemære (Bch.).
   978. Heandun (Ind.).
  1066. Heandune (Kble., Thorpe).
  1086. Handone (Dd.).
  1199} Hendon {(F.F.).
  1291}   {(T.E.).
          etc.

  A.S. æt ðǽre héan dúne, "at the high down or hill." *héan* is the inflected dative (weak decl.) after "æt" of A.S. *héah* (high).

Hercies Farm (Hillingdon).

  1532. Hersies (F.F.).

  Probably called after a man "Hercy." Cf. Walter Hercy mentioned in 1453 (F.F.).

Heston.

  c. 1180. Hestune (Dugd.).
  1200. Heston, Eston (Rot. c.r.).
  1227. Hestone (Cal. Rot. Ch.).
  1238}   {(F.F.).
  1291} Heston {(T.E.).
  1316}   {(F.A.).
  1544. Heeston (F.F.).

  Prefix may be A.S. *hése* (see *Hayes*). It is only a few miles from Hayes and in similar surroundings.

  For the second element see p. 106.

Highbury.

  c. 1370. Heybury (Gesta).
  1433} Highbury {(Dug.).
  1535}   {(V.E.)

1577.   Hiberie (Ind.).
1710.   Highbury Barn (Seller).
" the high stronghold or manor."   See p. 99.
M.E. high, hie, hey, hye, hyghe, etc.   See N.E.D.

HIGHGATE.

1391.   Heygate (F.F.).
1466⎫ Hygate ⎧(A.D.).
1478⎭   ⎩(Pat.).
1502.   Higate (A.D.).
1529.   Highgate (F.F.).

Lysons says : ". . . . the toll gate belonging to the bishop of London having stood from time immemorial on the summit of the hill."

HIGHWAY FARM (Harefield).

Marked in Rocque. It is situated on the road from Uxbridge to Harefield.

HIGHWOOD HILL (Edgeware).

1568.   Hyewoodhill (F.F.).
1596.   Highwood Hill (Norden).
        Cf. preceding names.

HILLINGDON.

1086.   Hillendone (Dd.).
1229.   Hillendon (F.F.).
1238.   Hilledon (F.F.).
1252.   Hillindone (Ind.).
1291.   Hilindon, Hillingdon (T.E.).
1306.   Hylendon (F.F.).
1388.   Hulynden (F.F.).
1452.   Helyngdon (F.F.).
1494.   Hillyngdon (F.F.).

The suffix -ing, though usually a patronymic, sometimes had the meaning of "dwellers in (on, at, by)." So that the sense may here be " down of the hill dwellers."

The surrounding country, except to the north, is nearly or quite dead level.

Searle, however, quotes one instance of a personal name " Hilla."

HITHERMOOR FARM (Staines).
No old forms.   Probably a new or imported name.

* HODFORD (Hampstead).
  1318.   Hodeford (F.F.).
  1398.   Hoddesford (Ch.).
  1535.   Hodford (V.E.).
" ford of Hod(d)or Hod(d)a."   Cf. *Hoddesdon* (Herts).
Hodford farm was recently demolished.   It was near Golders Green station.

HOLBORN (hoʊbɒn).
  1086.   Holeburne (Dd.).
  1197.   Holeburn, Holeborne (P.R.).
  1235.   Holleburn (F.F.).
  1291.   Holebourn, Holbourn (T.E.).
  1535.   Holborne (V.E.).
" stream in the hollow."   A.S. hol -e.

HOLLOWAY.
  1480.   Holwey (L.I., vol. 16).
  1486.   Holewey (Escaet).
  1535.   Holway (V.E.).
  1541.   Holwey (F.F.).
  1543.   Holowey (F.F.).
  1553.   Holwaye (F.F.).
  1554.   Hollowaye (F.F.).

"way lying in a hollow," cf. preceding. Modern form due to adjective "hollow" > A.S. *holh*. See N.E.D. "hole" and "hollow." The former hamlets of Upper and Lower Holloway were situated in a hollow between the villages of Highgate and Islington.

HOMERTON (Hackney).

   1343. Humburton (A.D.).
   1550. Humbarton (Stowe, vol. 2).
  1581, etc. Humberton, Hummerton (Mem.).
   1710. Humerton (Seller).

"farm or enclosure of Hunbeorht" [mb > nb by assimilation].

HORNSEY, HARRINGAY. (hɔːnzɪ, hærɪŋgeɪ).

Although these names present great difficulties, one thing is certain, viz. they are identical in origin.

Just as "chance" and "cadence" in French are both of the same origin, the one being the natural development of the Latin *cadentia, and the other being artificially introduced recently, so *Hornsey* seems to be the outcome through the mouths of the people and *Harringay* to be a fossilized or preserved form of the original name of the manor. I give a complete list of all spellings I have found without dividing into "types."

   1201. Haringue (F.F.).
  1216-1307. Heringeye (T.N.).
   1236. Harengheye (F.F.).
   1291. Haringeye (T.E.).
   1293. Haryngeye (F.F.).
  1272-1377. Heringeye (P.W.).
   1316. Harengey (F.A.).
   1341. Haringeye (F.F.).
   1346. Harengeye, Harngeye (F.F.).
   1351. Harngeye (Ch.).

1369, 1377 }
1373 } Haryngeseye { (F.F.).
{ (Close).

1381. Haryngey (F.F.).
1400. Harengey (A.D.).
1415. Haryngeay (A.D.).
1461. Harensey (F.F.).
1465. Haryngeay (F.F.).
1488. Haryngey, Harnyngey, Harnyssay (F.F.).
1530. Haryngay (F.F.).
1543, 1553. Harnesey (F.F.).
1556. Haryngey (F.F.).
1562. Haryngey otherwise Harnessey (F.F.).
1564. Hornsey (F.F.).
1610. Harnesey (Speed).
1710. Hornesey (Seller).
1862. Hornsey (village).   Haringey (name of manor house).   [Ordnance Map.]

The original name was, I think, a patronymic + ey (see p. 101).

There is no evidence that A.S. *hara*, "hare," was used as a personal name, but this was probably so as in the case of other animal names (cf. modern surname "Hare").

In Escaet, vol. I alone, I find Haringeby, Harington, Haringworthe, and in T.E. Harynton, Harynby, and the personal name Haryng. But the name may have been influenced later by the Norman name *Hareng*, cf. Ralph Hareng' (F.F., 1260).

The manor house name apparently retained its old form throughout, perhaps through the influence of documents or tradition. It survived till about 1870, and, when the house was demolished and the land built over, the district and the new station on the Great Northern main line became known as "Harringay."

The change from Haringey to Hornsey is hard to explain.

It must have taken place either through the form "Har-yngeseye," *harηze, *harnze, the *s* being perhaps introduced through the influence of the personal name "Hareng" (see above).

Or was the *g* at one time pronounced (dʒ)? There is a surname *Earengey* (ɩːrɪndʒeɪ) which might be derived from the place—cf. "Armitage," "Earnshaw." In that case the change may have been hareηge, hareηgje, hareηdje, har(ð)ndʒe, harndze, harnze.

Abinger (Surrey), *Bengeo* (Herts), and *Lockinge* (Berks), all have the sound (dʒ), and it is also common in Northumberland place names.

Prof. Mawer says: "If you are right in assuming a pronunciation with 'dge' at one stage . . . what you have in that case is one of the 'iggjo' stems in place of 'ingo.' . . ." Cf. the development of the modern Italian g (before e and i). Many of the spellings of the name above are of no help as the scribes in most instances would simply have copied from preceding documents, paying no attention to the changing pronunciation in the mouths of the inhabitants of the village. Most of the references would have been to the manor, which, as mentioned above, appears to have kept its original spelling and pronunciation throughout.

HORSENDON HILL (Sudbury).
    1203. Horsendun (F.F.).
    1261. Horsindune (A.D.).
    1819. Horsington Hill (Greenwood).
"down of Horsa, or of his sons." See pp. 100, 109.

HOUNDSDITCH.
  1216-1307. Hundesdich, Hondesdich (H.R.).
    1294. Hundesditch (Dug.).
Cf. following name. A.S. *dic* meant both a "ditch" and "dike." Here probably the former.

HOUNSLOW.

1086.   Honeslauu (Dd.).

1216-1307 }
1316 }   Hundeslawe { (T.N.), (H.R.).
                      { (F.A.).

1327-1377 }
1446 }   Houndeslowe { (N.I.).
                       { (Ind.).

1535.   Hounslowe (V.E.).

" mound or tumulus of Hund."   See p. 105.

The literal meaning of Hund is " dog," but here used as a personal name as the genitival " s " shows.

Cf. " *On hundes hlœw.*"   (A.D. 953, Kemble, vol. V, p. 325.)

HOXTON.

1086.   Hochestone (Dd.).
1221.   Hocston (F.F.).
1291.   Hoxton (T.E.).
1352.   Hoggeston (Close).
1371.   Hogeston (F.F.).
1533.   Hoggeston (F.F.).
1545.   Hoxton (F.F.).

" farm or enclosure of Hocg."

* HYDE (Halliford).

1314.   Hide (F.F.).
1369.   Hyde (F.F.).

HYDE (Hendon).

Marked in maps from seventeenth century, cf. above.

HYDE (Hyde Park).

1204.   Hida (F.F.).

1257 }
1306 }   Hyde { (F.F.).
               { (F.F.).

1596.   Hyde Park (Norden).

A.S. híd, hígid, " a hide "—a certain measure of land of variable extent, generally estimated at 100 to 120 acres.

ICKENHAM.

      1086.   Ticheham (Dd.).

1163, etc.   Tichehā (P.R.).

      1205.   Tĭkehā (F.F.).

      1206.   Ykeham (F.F.).

      1252 } Ikenham { (Ch.).

      1291 }   { (T.E.).

      1300.   Tykenham (I.p.m.).

      1316.   Ikenham (F.A.).

The first element is a personal name Ticca.

For second element see p. 103.

Loss of initial " t " due to influence of preposition " at," cf. *Elstree* and *Oakington*.

ISLE OF DOGS.

    Isle of Doggs (Seller).   Isle of Dogges (Speed).

    Origin of name uncertain.   Various conjectures are given in " O. and N.," vol. I, pp. 533-537.   There may have been kennels here at one time, chosen as a suitable spot by some former sovereign or lord.

ISLEWORTH (aɪzðl-).

      1086.   Gistelesworde (Dd.).

      1179.   Ysteleswurde (P.R.).

1216-1307.   Istelesworth, Istleworth (H.R.).

      1291.   Istelwrth (T.E.).

      1305.   Yiselworthe, Yistelworth (F.F.).

      1330.   Istelesworde (Ch.).

      1333.   Yistilworth (F.F.).

      1428.   Istelworth (F.A.).

      1610.   Thistleworth (Speed).

      1754.   Isleworth (Rocque).

The first element is a personal name * *Gistel* (the persistent *t* is against derivation from A.S. *gisl*, " hostage," as first

4 *

element).   * *Gistel* might be an extension of *Gist*.   Searle
has a " Gistheard."

For the second element see p. 107.

ISLINGTON.

1086.	Iseldone, Isendone (Dd.).
1197.	Iseldon (P.R.).
1220.	Ysendon (F.F.).

1216-1307		(T.N.).
1282		(Escaet).
1291, 1316	Iseldon	(T.E., F.A.).
Up to 1500		(F.F. *passim*).

1503.	Islyngton (F.F.).
1535.	Iselden, Islyngton (V.E.).
1558-1603.	Isledon *alias* Islington (Proc. Chanc Eliz.).

There is no sign of the *ing* till the sixteenth century.   It
seems to have been inserted then for no particular reason.
The type Isen- may mean " iron hill " (because of its mineral
springs ?), or *Isen* may stand for * *Isena*(n), short for one of
the A.S. personal names beginning with *Isen* (" iron ").   The
type *Isel-* must be due, I think, to dissimilation, for A.S. *gisl*,
" hostage," or a personal name *Gisla*, would give an initial
y in M.E.—at least in some forms.   Lysons states that
" Isendune " occurs in the most ancient records belonging to
the Church of St. Paul's, so we may consider that form to
be the original type.

KEMPTON.

1086.	Cheneton (Dd.).
1216-1307.	Keninton, Kenynton (T.N.).
1228.	Keninton (Ch.).
1293.	Keneton (I.p.m.).
1328.	Kenyngton (Close).
1407, 1421.	Coldekenyngton (F.F.).

1610, 1754.   Kenton (Speed, Rocque).

1819.   Kempton (Greenwood).

" farm of the sons of Cena or Coena."   See pp. 106, 108.

A comparison of the old forms shows that *Kempton*, *Kenton* (*infra*) and *Kennington* (Surrey) are all of the same origin, so that it is curious that their modern forms are so different.

KENSAL GREEN.

1557.   Kellsell Grene (Harl. MS., No. 62, fol. 46 b).[1]

1756.   Kensel Grene (Rocque).

Since the place was insignificant, I think it must be named after a man Kelshull (Kelshelle, Kelshill, etc.).   This personal name occurs frequently in old records (as in A.D.) and is, I suppose, from Kelshall (Herts), formerly Kelshulle, Kelshille, etc.

n > l through dissimilation.

KENSINGTON.

1086.   Chenesitun (Dd.).

1235.   Kensington (F.F.).

1264.   Kensenton (I.p.m.).

1284.   Kensintone (Ind.).

1291.   Kensington (T.E.).

" farm of the sons of Cynesige."   The *g* being a mere glide would drop out.   In fact, Searle gives late forms of the name Chinesi, Chenisi.

The sound (η) was difficult to the Normans.   They either dropped it, or represented it by n (sometimes by *g* or *nc*).

KENTISH TOWN.

1208.   Kentisston (F.F.).

1227.   Kentissetone (Cal. Rot. Ch.).

1282.   Kenteston (Escaet).

---

[1] For this information I am indebted to my friend, Mr. R. Coates of the MSS. Dept. Brit. Mus.

1291.   Kentisshetune (T.E.).
1301.   Kentissetown (F.F.).
1316.   Kentyssheton (F.A.).
1535.   Kentishe Towne (V.E.).

" Kentish farm " (A.S. centisc).   Histories give no clue to the reason for the epithet.   Perhaps the original owner came from or had other property in Kent.

It is curious that the original form should have come down so unchanged.   Cf. *Ken Wood.*

KENTON (Harrow).
1232.   Keninton (F.F.).
1368.   Kenyngton next Harogh' (F.F.).
1596.   Kenton (Norden).

Same origin as *Kempton* q.v.

KEN WOOD (Highgate).
?1434.   Kentwode (F.F.).
1558-1579.   Caen Wood (L.I., vol. 7).
1603-1625 } Cane Wood { (L.I., vol. 25).
1695 } { (Camden).
1754.   Ken Wood (Rocque).

Uncertain.

Histories give little help, but suggest that the name may come from Reginald de Kentewode, a dean of Westminster. The converse is, however, possible.   Cf. Kentish Town nearby.

KILBURN.
c. 1150.   Kyneburna, Cuneburna, Keneburna (Dug.).
1208.   Keleburne, Kelebirne (F.F.).
1229.   Kylleborne (Dug.)
1236 } Keleburn { (F.F.).
1306 } { (Ind.).
1340.   Kellebourn (F.F.).

1354.   Kilbourn (Pat.).
1525.   Kylbourne (F.F.).
1535.   Kilborne, Kylborne (V.E.).
Kelle-, Kele-, Kille-, Kil-, Kyl-, etc.   F.F., Dug. .

If the earliest forms are to be trusted the meaning was " bourn or stream of Cȳna." See p. 99.

The later forms may represent a type * Cyllan burna, " bourn of Cylla," but the *l* may be due to dissimilation.   Cf. *Islington*.

KINGSBURY.

966.   æt Cyngesbyrig (Kble.).
1044.   Kynges byrig (Ind.).
1086.   Chingesberie (Dd.).
1200.   Kingesbir' (Rot. C.R.).
1316.   Kyngesbury (F.A.).
" at the King's stronghold."   See p. 99.
Cf. *Kingston* (Surrey).   *Cyningestune* in the Chronicle.

KINGS END (Ruislip).
1710.   Kings End (Seller).

Here " King" was probably a man's name.   See also p. 101.

KINGSLAND (Hackney).
1550 ⎫   ⎧(Stow).
1581 ⎬ Kingsland ⎨(Mem.).
1636 ⎭   ⎩(Middlesex and Herts Queries).

This place name, which is found elsewhere in England, generally referred to land held by the king as opposed to the church.

KITTS END (Hadley).
1545, 1569.   Kyckes ende (F.F.).
Kyck or Kitt was probably the name of a man.
c and *t* easily interchange.

KNIGHTSBRIDGE.

    c. 1220.   Cnichtebrugg (Ind.).
    1261.   Knyttebrugg (F.F.).
    1270.   Knichtebrugg (I.M.).
    1305.   Knyghtebregg (F.F.).
    1364.   Knyghtesbrugg (F.F.).
    1393.   Knightesbrigge (Escaet).

    A.S. * cnihta brycg, " bridge of the ' Knights,' " " knight " having its original sense of " servant," " boy," " serving boy or man."

    There is a *cnihta bryge* in Kble., but not referring to this place.

KNIGHTSCOTE FARM (Harefield).

    1367.   Knyghtecote (A.D.).
    1404.   Knyghtcotes (F.F.).

    Cf. preceding and see p. 100.

KNOWLE GREEN (Staines).

    So spelt in Rocque.   Knowl Green in Seller.

    M.E. *knol,* " hill," " mount " (A.S. cnol).   Often applied to a small round hill.

LALEHAM.

    1062.   Lælham (Kble.).
    1086.   Leleham (Dd.).
    1207   ⎱   (F.F.).
    1256   ⎰ Lalham ⎱ (F.F.).
    1274   (F.F.).
    1291   ⎰   (T.E).
    1328.   Laleham (Ch.).
1332, 1355.   Lalham (F.F.).
    1467.   Laleham (F.F.).

    There is no name like this in Searle.   Perhaps the prefix

is A.S. *læl*, " twig," " withy," " switch," etc., referring to certain plants by the river there, used as such.

Johnstone assumes an unrecorded personal name *Lela* as
the prefix.

LAMPTON (Hounslow).

    1375}   Lamptonfeld {(Close).
    1376}   {(A.D.).
    1754. Lampton (Rocque).

Probably " lamb farm."   [pt > bt is normal.]

See *field* and *ton*, pp. 101, 106.   Cf. *Lambton* (Northumberland), which has some early forms, " Lampton."

LEA (river).

        891. Lyga (Chron.).
        896. Liggean, Lygean (Chron.).
        913. Ligean (Chron.).
 1216-1307. Luyam (H.R.).
      1313. Luye (Plac. Abb.).
      1319. aqua vocata la Leye (Ind.).
                    Leye, Ley, Lea subsq.

Of doubtful origin, possibly a pre-Celtic. $\sqrt{}$lyg [phonetic].
Modern spelling is due to association with *ley*, *lea* (meadow).
It was probably never pronounced [le:].

LIMEHOUSE.

    1367} les lymostes {(Cor.).
    1405}   {(A.D.).
    1496. Lymost (F.F.).
    1535. Lymehurst (V.E.).
    1547. Lymehouse (F.F.).

" Lime oasts " (A.S. ást), i.e. oasts or kilns for burning lime
in.   Modern outcome due to popular etymology.

"LISSON GREEN."

    1086.   Lilestone (Dd.).
    1198⎫
    1237⎬ Lilleston ⎧(Fees).
    1240⎭   ⎨(Ch.).
                      ⎩(F.F.).
    1561.   Lylleston (F.F.).
    1695.   Lising Green (Camden).
    1795.   Lisson Green (Lysons).

"farm or enclosure of Lil(le)."

1st < ls < ss, cf. Sipson.   ls > 1st due to simplification.

The village of Lisson Green lay between Paddington and Marylebone and was absorbed into London, *c.* 1830. The name remains in " Lisson Grove."

LITTLETON.

Type I.

    1184.   Litleton (P.R.).
    1204.   Lutleton (F.F.).
    1282.   Littilton (F.F.).
    1291.   Litleton (T.E.).
    1310.   Littleton (F.F.).
    1467.   Litilton (F.F.).
    1469.   Lytellton (F.F.).

Type II.

  1216-1307.   Litlinton (T.N.).
  1327-1377.   Litelynton (N.I.).
    1328.   Litlyngton (Close).
    1341.   Lutilynton (F.F.).
    1347.   Lutelyngton (F.F.).
    1350.   Letelyngton (Cal. Rot. Ch.).
    1356.   Litlyngton (F.F.).
    1428.   Lytlyngton (F.A.).
  1558-1603.   Litleton al. Litlington (Proc. Chanc. Eliz.)

Type I. = "little farm or enclosure."   *Type II.* = " farm of the Lytlingas or sons of Lytel " (Little). Modern form from *Type I*.

LONGFORD.

1327 }
1343 } Langeford { (F.F.).
             { (Rot. Abb.).
1402. Langford (A.D.).
1430. Longford, Longforthe (F.F.).

" long ford," referring to the many branches of the Colne here.

LOTHBURY (in the City).

1181-1203. Lodebure (quoted Harben).
1232. Lothebiri (Ch.).
1291. Lotheber', Lothesber' (T.E.).
1374. Lothbury (Escaet).

For the second element, see p. 99.

The first element is a personal name *Hlōþa, short for some name Hloþgar, Hloþhere, Hloþwig, etc. (Luther, Louis).

LUDGATE (a City gate).

1100-1135. Lutgata (Harben).
1216-1307. Ludgate (H.R.).
1272. Ludegate (Ch.).
1291. Ludgate, Lutgate (T.E.).
1312. Lutgate (F.F.).
1535. Ludgate (V.E.).

I can suggest no sound interpretation. Absence of any forms with *i* is against derivation from A.S. *hludgeat* (" swing-gate ").

MAIDA VALE (Kilburn).

Maida Hill, 1819 (Greenwood). M. Vale is a " back formation." Named after the battle of Maida (1806).

MARE STREET (Hackney).

  1596, 1610. Mere Street (Norden, Speed).

   1710. Mare Street (Seller).

"Street" may here have the sense of "scattered hamlet."
See p. 105. "Mere" probably had reference to some neigh-
bouring pool.

MARYLEBONE ('mærɪlðbðn).

   1490 { . . . Manor of Tyborne, otherwise } (F.F.).
                  called Maryborne

   1492 } Marybourne { (A.D.).
   1511 }   { (F.F.).

   1535. Mariborne (V.E.).

   1543 } Maribone { (Dug.).
   1623 }   { (Ind.).

   1754. Mary le Bone (Rocque).

Now usually understood as meaning "Mary the good," but
the original suffix was "bourn" (a stream) and the *le* is of
quite recent introduction, perhaps due to such names as
"Mary le Strand," etc.

   Originally known as Tyburn (q.v.), the name was changed,
owing to the church on the banks dedicated to the Virgin.
Cf. "Land in the parish of the Blessed Mary of Marybourne"
(F.F., 1511).

MAYFAIR. See p. 96.

MIDDLESEX.

   704. in provincia quae nuncupatur Middelseaxan
              (Bch., Kble.).

   767. in Middil Saexum (Bch., Kble.).

  c. 970. on Middel Seaxan (Kble.).

   998. in Middilsexan (Thorpe).

   1011. Middelseaxe, Middelsexe, Middelsexa (Chron.).

  c. 1060. on Middelsexan (Kble.).

   1086. Midelsexe (Dd.).

   1154. Middelsexe, Middelsex (P.R.).

" the middle Saxons," as opposed to east, west and south S. The actual boundaries, however, were not yet formed by 704 A.D. There were two declensions of the word " Saxons " in A.S. (1) a weak plural *Seaxan*. (2) a plural Seaxe-a-um. This latter type of declension was used in A.S. in the names of certain tribes as *Dene, Engle, Suþrige* (Surrey), etc. See Wright's " Old English Grammar."

The root of the name " Saxons " is generally held to be the word " *seax*," " knife," " sword," cognate with Latin *saxum*.

MILE END (Stepney).
>   14th century.   Milende (Gesta).
>   1349.   Mylende (L.I., vol. 6).
>   1405.   Mileshende (A.D.).
>   1437.   Mile End (F.F.).

So called, according to histories, because distant one mile from Aldgate, on the road to Colchester, etc., eastwards.

MILL HILL (Hendon).
>   1596.   Mylhill (Norden).

I have found no earlier forms.   Meaning obvious.

MILLWALL (Poplar).
Marsh Wall in Rocque.   Mill Wall, Millwall in nineteenth century maps.   Named, according to histories, after seven mills which stood here along the river bank.

MIMMS (South).
>   1086.   Mimes (Dd.).
>   1210 ⎫   ⎧ (R.E.).
>   1216-1307 ⎪ Mimmes ⎪ (T.N.).
>   1268 ⎬   ⎨ (I.p.m.).
>   1291 ⎭   ⎩ (T.E.).
>   1255.   Suthmimmes (F.F.).
>   1312.   Suthmymmes (Ch.).
>   etc.

Doubtful. Perhaps the Mimmas were some small tribe or family otherwise unknown.

North Mimms (Herts) has similar old forms, except Dd., which is *Mimmene*—? gen. plur. of a corresponding weak declension *Mimman*.

MOORHALL FARM (Harefield).

    1395. Morhalle (F.F.).

    1535⎱
    1553⎰ Morehall ⎰(V.E.).
                   ⎱(F.F.).

The prefix is "moor," which had however in A.S. the meaning of "wet swampy land," and this suits the situation of the place. The suffix may be "hall," but is possibly "hale." Cf. the M.E. forms of *Northall* and *Southall*. See *Hale*, p. 102.

MUSWELL HILL.

    1152-1160. Mosewella (Ind.).

    1535. Muswell (V.E.).

    1541. Mossewell (Dug.).

    1544. Muswell (F.F.).

"mossy well or spring." A.S. *méos* often gave *mose* in M.E., whence mus [ŏ-ŭ-u].

Johnston says "*Muswell Hill*—Old Mustwell . . .," but I have not come across this form.

NEASDEN.

    ‡ (?) 939. Neasdune (Bch.).

    ‡ (?) 939. Neosdune (Kble.).

    1291. Nesdon (T.E.).

    1300. Nesedon (A.D.).

    1322. Nesdone (A.D.).

    1535. Nesdon, Neesdon (V.E.).

    1610. Nesedon (Speed).

For the second element, see p. 100.

The first element is M.E. nes, nese (neose, nease, nees, neese) = "*nose*," also "*ness*," cognate with Mid. Dutch and Mid. Low. Ger. *nese*. See *nese* in N.E.D., also nose, naze and ness, all of which words are probably related. A.S. had only *nes* and *næs*, according to N.E.D., but the earliest forms above are probably post-conquest copies.

The name *Neasden*, therefore, may refer to a hill jutting out like a "nose" into the plain. Cf. *Nesbit* (Northumberland).

NORTHOLT.
    962.   æt norð healum (Earle, p. 202, Thorpe).
    1086.   Northala (Dd.).
    1210 } Northale { (R.E.).
    1231 }   { (F.F.).
    1213.   Northal (F.F.).
    1291.   Northall (T.E.).
    1399.   Northalle (A.D.).
    1596.   Northold (Norden).
    1610.   Northolt (Speed).

Originally "north hale" as opposed to "Southall" (q.v.). See *hale*, p. 102.

The additional *d* or *t* is not due to the influence of the word "holt," which does not occur in Middlesex except in *Wormholt*, but is simply parasitic. Cf. *sound* in N.E.D. and the vulgar "gownd" for gown.

NORTH HYDE (Southall).
    1243.   Northyde (F.F.).
    1356.   Northide (F.F.).
    1710.   Northhide (Seller).
from "north" and "hide"—see *Hyde* (*supra*).

NORTHWOOD.
1438, 1462.   Northwode, Northwod (Pat.). Because it lay to the North of Ruislip.

NORTON FOLGATE (Shoreditch).

1307⎫ Norton ⎧(F.F.).
1324⎭   ⎩(F.F.).
1433. Nortonfolyot (F.F.).
1458. Nortonfoly (F.F.).
1520. Norton Folyott (F.F.).
1542. Norton Folgate, otherwise Norton Follyott (F.F.).

"north farm." It was just north of the City walls.

According to Johnston there are twenty-two Nortons in the Post Office Directory alone.

Foliott is a Norman family name (diminutive of fon, fol, "mad," according to Prof. Weekley), cf. *Tamerton Foliott* (Devon).

The modern *Folgate* is due to the influence of the numerous City gates.

NORWOOD GREEN.

1294. Northwode (F.F.).
1453. Norwode (A.D.).

The modern outcome is the normal one, *Northwood* (*supra*) being unusual.

NOTTING (Kensington).

1476. Knottinge Bernes (Escaet).
1519. Notingbarns (F.F.).
1544. Nuttingbars (F.F.).
1754. Knotton Barn (Rocque).
1862. Notting Barns Farm (6-inch ordnance map).

"Place of the Cnottingas or sons of Cnotta." Cf. *Knotting* (Beds) and *Knottingley* (Yorks).

Notting Hill and Notting Dale are back formations from this place. Notting Hill Gate—because a turnpike stood here on the main road from London to Oxford.

OAKINGTON FARM (Wembley).

1236 ⎫
1240 ⎬ Tokinton ⎰ (Rot. Abb.).
        ⎱ (F.F.).

1508 ⎫
1535 ⎬ Tokyngton ⎰ (F.F.).
          ⎱ (V.E.).

1819.   Oakington farm (Greenwood).

"farm of the sons of Tōca."

For loss of initial *t*, cf. Elstree and Ickenham, but the loss must have occurred quite recently in this case.

OLD FOLD FARM (Barnet).

c. 1340.   Le Eldefolde (Gesta).

1539.   Oldfelde (F.F.).

1754.   Old Fold (Rocque).

See p. 101 and cf. the following.

OLD FORD ('ould 'fɔ: d).

1349.   Eldeford (L.I., vol. 6).

1383.   Oldeford (Escaet).

1384.   Oldforthe (F.F.).

1400.   Oldford (F.F.).

A.S. æt ðám ealdan forda, "at the old ford"—probably as opposed to *Stratford*, lower down.

There is no apparent reason for writing the name in two words. The normal outcome should be "Oldford" ('ouldfɔd).

OSSULSTON (name of a Hundred).

1086.   Osulvestan (Dd.).

1168, 1187.   Osulfestan (P.R.).

1200.   Osulvestan (Rot. C.R.).

1216-1307.   Othulveston (H.R.).

1428.   Osulveston (F.A.).

1610.   Ossulston (Speed).

"at the stone of Oswulf."   See p. 105.

For loss of *v* cf. Elstree, Harlesden, etc.

OSTERLEY PARK (Hounslow).

  1294. Osterlye (F.F.).
  1342. Oysterley (Pat.).
  1351. Osterlee (Ch.).
  1376. Osturle (A.D.).
  1460. Osterley (Escaet).

Prof. Mawer considers the first element to be A.S. *eowistre*, " a sheepfold " [ewe], which he and Dr. Bradley " agree now is the derivation of Durham ' Ousterley '."

I can suggest no alternative, and the form *oy* (above) favours A.S. "*eowistre*."

OXGATE FARM (Hendon).

  1291 } Oxegate { (T.E.).
  1311 }   { (F.F.).
  1535. Oxgate (V.E.).
      Cf. the following.

OXHEYLANE FARM (Pinner).

 Called after *Oxhey* (Herts).

  1007. æt Oxangehæge (Crawford).
  1219. Oxehaie (F.F.).
  1248. Oxehaye (F.F.).

" Enclosed or fenced in place of Oxen."

PADDINGTON.

  ‡959. Padintune (Kble., Thorpe).
  ‡998. Paddingtone (Thorpe).
 1168, 1169. Padinton (P.R.).
  c. 1220. Padintune (Ind.).
  1377. Padyngton (A.D.).
  1610. Paddington (Speed).

" farm of the sons of Pada or Padda."

 Cf. Padingdene in F.A., 1316 = Paddington farm, Abinger (Surrey).

PAGE STREET (Hendon).

     1710.   Page Street (Seller).

See *street*, p. 105.   The name "Page" occurs frequently in the F.F.

* "PALLINGSWICK," "PADDINGSWICK" (Ealing).

     1270.   Palyngewýk (F.F.).

 1364, 1373.   Palyngeswiche (Close).

     1380.   Pallyngeswyk (Ind.).

     1391.   Pallingwike (Escaet).

     1486.   Palyngeswyke (Escaet).

     1547.   Palenswyke otherwise Padenswyke (F.F.).

     1819.   Padderswick Green (Greenwood).

(?) "dwelling of the son(s) of * Pala."   This name, however, is not in Searle, and it is possible that the prefix is a personal name Pallig or Palling(us), *Pallig* being the name of a Danish earl (Searle).   But *Pallinsburn* (Northumberland) = "bourn of Paulinus."

For interchange of *l* and *d*, cf. *Charlton* and *Harlington*.

PALMERS GREEN (Edmonton).

    ? 1205.   Palmeresfeld . . . in Edelmeton (F.F.).

     1695.   Palmers Green (Camden).

Palmer = "pilgrim to the Holy Land."   See "Romance of Names" (Weekley), pp. 15, 167.

PARSONS GREEN (Fulham).

     1596.   Parsons Grene (Norden).

So called, according to Lysons, because the parsonage house of Fulham stood here, round which the hamlet grew up.

PENTONHOOK (Laleham).

     1535.   Pentyhoke (F.F.).

"hook," referring to the point of land running into the Thames here.

For want of early forms I cannot interpret the prefix.

5 *

PENTONVILLE (Islington).

Named after Henry Penton (*ob.* 1812). He owned the land, and laid out the first streets in 1773 (Besant).

PERIVALE.

1508, 1566.   Pyryvale (F.F.).
     1564.   Peryvale (F.F.).
     1568.   Perevell (F.F.).

Prefix is probably M.E. pery, piry, pirie, "pear tree" (A.S. pìriȝe). The French suffix -vale shows that the place is of post-conquest origin. It was, in fact, known as "Little Greenford" till the fifteenth century.

PERRY OAKS.

     1404.   Godfrey atte Pyrye (F.F.).
     1411.   Pyrye (A.D.).
     1553.   Puryplace (F.F.).
     1754.   Perry Oaks (Rocque).

Prefix as in preceding name. The "Oaks" is fairly modern.

PIELD HEATH (Cowley).

     1636.   Peel's Heath (quoted Lysons).
     1754.   Peel Heath (Rocque).

I suppose "*Peel*" to have been a man's name. The modern "d" is excrescent.

PIMLICO.

     c. 1626.   Pimlico, Pimplico, Pimlicoe (quoted Clinch's
             "History of Mayfair and Belgravia").
     1754.   Pimlico (Rocque).

The name, according to histories, seems to come from a certain Ben Pimlico, who had a tavern. I suppose it to be of foreign origin.

PINKWELL (Harlington).

So spelt in Rocque, but no earlier forms that I can find.

There is a *Pinca* in Searle, and cf. *Pinkhurst* (Surrey) spelt *Pinkehurst* in the Surrey Fines, 1241 and 1356.

PINNER.

1232.	Pinora (F.F.).
1232.	Pinnora (Ch.).
1248.	Pinnore (S.S., vol. 2).
1255.	Pinhore (F.F.).
1332.	Pinnere (Ind.).
1532.	Pynner (F.F.).

The suffix is A.S. *ora*, "brim," "edge," "bank," "shore," referring to the little river *Pin* here.

I think, however, that the river name must be a back formation, and the prefix represent a personal name *Pinna*. Cf. "Pinnan rod" in Searle.

A.S. *ora* becomes -or -er in place names when a suffix, and in all cases is pronounced [ɒ(r)].

PITSHANGER (Ealing).

1538, 1563.	Pytteshanger (F.F.).
1754.	Pitshanger Lane (Rocque).
1819.	Pitch hanger Farm (Greenwood).

For suffix, cf. *Hanger Hill* (*supra*).

Prefix evidently a proper name, but uncertain what without earlier forms, since *t* and *c* so readily interchange. Perhaps the surname *Pitt*, if the name is really modern.

POLEHILL FARM (Hillingdon).

Pole Hill Farm in Greenwood.

Perhaps "pool hill," but it may be an imported name.

PONDERS END (Enfield).

1610.	Ponder's End (Speed).

See p. 101. "Ponder," I suppose to have been a man's name.

* PONTEFRACT, POMFRET (a former manor by the Thames).
    1308.   Pontefract (F.F.).
    1323.   Ponfrayt super Thamisiam (Escaet).
    1358.   Pountfreyt (F.F.).
    1370.   Pomfreit (Escaet).
    1422.   Pountfreit (F.F.).
"broken bridge," cf. *Pontefract* (Yorks).

The first form is an artificial Latin one; the rest Norman French, cf. *Grampound* (Cornwall), Grauntpont, Grauntpond (Ind., 1422), i.e. "great bridge" (over the river Fal).

POPLAR.
    1340 ⎫
    1351 ⎬ Popeler ⎰ (F.F.).
    1405 ⎭   ⎱ (Escaet).
                    (A.D.).
    1398.   Popellier (F.F.).
    1569.   Popler (A.D.).
"at the poplar tree," cf. *Eyke, Elm, Ash, Thorne, Wellow*, etc., in various counties.

This name occurs earlier than the first record of the word in the N.E.D. (1382).

* PORTOBELLO FARM (Notting Hill).
Marked in eighteenth and nineteenth century maps down to *c.* 1870.

Named, according to histories in honour of the capture of Portobello in 1739. The name remains in the Portobello Road, formerly a lane leading to the farm.

* PORTPOOL (a lost manor near the present Gray's Inn, London).
    c. 1200 ⎫ Purtepol ⎰ (Excerpta).
    1203 ⎭   ⎱ (F.F.).
    c. 1220 ⎫ Purtepole ⎰ (Ind.).
    1309 ⎭   ⎱ (F.F.).

1316. Pourtepol (F.A.).
1507. Portpole (F.F.).
1535. Portepole, Portepoole (V.E.).

the " u " shows that the prefix cannot be " port " in any sense of the word, but rather a personal name " Purta " (ı in Searle). Cf. *Purtanige* in Kble.

POTTERS BAR.

1596. Potters Barr (Norden).

So called because formerly one of the "bars" or barred gates of Enfield Chase.

Potter was the name of an underkeeper of one of the lodges, which was known as " Potter's Lodge " in 1635 (G.L.).

POYLE.

1210. Pulla (R.E.).
1216-1307. Puilla (T.N.).
1238. Poyle (F.F.).
1259. la Puille (F.F.).
1452. Poyle (Escaet).

From the Norman family name Poille, Puille.

Poyle comes from the form Poille, whereas Pewley Hill (near Guildford, Surrey) comes from Puille—like "pew" > old French "puy." See V.C.H., Surrey, vol. 3.

PRESTON (Harrow).

1210. Prestone (R.E.).
1232 } Preston { (F.F.).
1596 }   { (Norden).

" farm of the priests," A.S. * preosta tún. A common place name in England.

Prestone and Preostantun in Kble. refer, I think, not to this place, but to somewhere in Hants.

PRIMROSE HILL.

Marked in Rocque and mentioned in the seventeenth century, according to histories. Probably descriptive of its former appearance.

RATCLIFF (Stepney).
   1422. Radclif (F.F.).
   1430. Radclyf (F.F.).
   1541. Radclyff, Ratclyff (S.S., vol. 8).
   1573. Redcliffe (Mid. Ped.).
   1593. Ratcliff (A.D.)
" red cliff," the *d* becoming voiceless before the *c*.

The notorious " Ratcliff Highway " formerly preserved the name.

RAVENSCOURT PARK (Hammersmith).

Raven's Court in Greenwood. Only dates from the eighteenth century, but the name Raven is old, having been used as a personal name in A.S.

A patronymic is seen in *Ravenyngemill* (F.F., 1404).

RED HILL (Edgeware).

So marked in Seller (1710). I suppose from a certain colour of the clay soil here, cf. *Redhill* (Surrey).

" ROKESHAL."
   1214. Rokeshal (F.F.).
" nook or corner of Hrŏc." See *Hale* and cf. following.

This name is perhaps represented by *Ruckhold Farm* near Harlesden, cf. *Northolt* (*supra*).

ROXETH.
   845. et (= æt) Hroces seaðum (Bch.).
   845. Hroces seað (Ind.).
   1422. Roxhethe (F.F.).
   1508. Roxehay (F.F.).
   1710. Roxeth (Seller).

A.S. *seað* meant " a pit, hole, well, lake." See p. 105.

Prefix is a personal name Hrōc (= Rook), rather than the bird itself, owing to the presence of the genitival -*es*.

* RUDSWORTH (Staines ?).

      1243. Ruddeswurth (F.F.).

      1258. Rudesworth (F.F.).

1279, 1446. Rodesworth (F.F.).

      1391. Rodesworthe (Escaet).

      1464. Ruddesworth (Pat.).

      1466. Ruddisworth (F.F.).

"farm or holding of * Rud(d)." The weak Ruda is in Searle.

* RUGMERE (St. Pancras, a lost manor near).

      1086. Rugemere (Dd.).

      1291. Rugmē (T.E.).

1327-1377. Reggemē (N.I.).

      1535. Rugmer (V.E.).

Presumably " ridge mere." A.S. *hrycg* (i.e. ridge or back). The letter " e " is a Kentish symbol and the letter " u " is a Norman symbol for the sound of A.S. " y."

RUISLIP (raɪslɪp).

      1086. Rislepe (Dd.).

      1230. Rislep (F.F.).

      1246   Risselep   (S.S., vol 2).

      1252   (Ch.).

      1291. Russelep (T.E.).

      1307. Risshelep, Rysshelep (F.F.).

      1315. Rushlep (F.F.).

1327-1377. Russhelep (N.I.).

      1434. Ruyssheleppe (L.I., vol. 5).

      1436. Ruyslyp (Escaet).

. 1438, 1462. Ruyslep, Ruyslepe (Pat.).

      1506. Ryselypp (F.F.).

The prefix is A.S. risce, rysce (risc, rysc), " a rush."

The suffix is A.S. hlyp, hlep, " a leaping place," " distance to be leaped over," referring to the small stream (the Pin) here which flows into the Colne.

The *ui* represents a M.E. spelling of the sound of A.S. y (= French " u "), cf. buy, build, bruise, etc., in N.E.D.

The sound was later " unrounded " according to rule, but the spelling remains.

RYEFIELDS BARN.

Marked in Seller, 1710.   Probably to be interpreted literally.

ST. GILES.

1204, 1247 ⎫ St. Gyles ⎰ (F.F.).
1257, 1519 ⎭   ⎱ (A.D.).
     1565.   St. Giles in the Fields (F.F.).

The village and church were named after the hospital which stood here, dedicated to the Greek saint, St. Giles.

ST. JOHNS WOOD.

     1577.   St. Johns Wood (Ind.).

The wood was in the possession of the Priors of St. John of Jerusalem.

ST. PANCRAS.

     1086.   (ad) Sanctum Pancratium (Dd.).
     1183.   eccl. S. Pancratii (Ind.).
     1291.   Sc̃i Pancratii (T.E.).
     1353.   de Sancti Pancrassi (F.A.).
     1428.   Ecc. Sancti Pancracii (F.A.).

" Pancratius " was a young Phrygian nobleman, who suffered martyrdom under Diocletian, and was at one time a favourite saint in England.   Cf. *St. Pancras* (Sussex).

SANDFORD HOUSE (Fulham).

1185⎤
1272⎦ Sandford {(Ind.).
                {(F.F.).

SCRATTAGE (Hounslow).

1710, 1754.   Scratedge (Seller, Rocque).

No earlier forms that I can find, but the suffix is possibly "edge."   Cf. *Gutteridge* (*supra*).

SHACKLEWELL (Hackney).

1550.   Shakelwell (Stow).

1553.   Shackewell (F.F.).

1581, etc.   Shacklewell (Mem.).

c. 1600.   Shackelwell (Mid. Ped.).

Might be "well by which beasts or people were shackled." So Walker interprets *Shacklecross* (Derbyshire).

But *Shackleford* (Surrey) was Saklesford in 1229 (Surrey Fines), pointing to a personal name * Sceacul.

Prof. Weekley quotes a Robert Schakel in 1297 (Surnames) and Shackle is still found as a surname.

SHADWELL.

1223.   Shadewell (F.F.).

1316.   Shaldewelle (Ch.).

1325.   Shadewell (Plac. Abb.).

"Shallow well or spring."   Loss of *l* after *a* and before *d* is Norman, though this was often rendered *au*.   Cf. *Adewych* in F.F., 1237 = Aldwych, and *Chaldewell*, F.F., 1318, now *Chadwell* (Essex).

SHEEPCOTE FARM (Harrow).

1399.   Schepcote (Escaet).

1422.   Shipcote (Escaet).

1710.   Sheepcoate (Seller).

See p. 100.   Probably a shepherd's dwelling.

The 1422 form represents the normal outcome of the name.

SHEPHERD's BUSH (Hammersmith)

    1710.   Shepards Bush (Seller).

A small hamlet till the nineteenth century. Shepard (i.e. " Shepherd ") was probably a man's name. It occurs several times in F.F.

SHEPPERTON.

‡ 959, 1066 ⎫
   ‡ 1066 ⎭ Scepertune ⎰ (Thorpe).
                      ⎱ (Ind.).

   ‡ 1066.   Scepirton (Kble.).

   1086.   Scepertune (Dd.).

   1208.   Sceperton (F.F.).

   1297 ⎫
   1309 ⎭ Sheperton ⎰ (Pat.).
                    ⎱ (F.F.).

   1316.   Scheperton (F.A.).

   1393.   Sheperton (Escaet).

For the second element see p. 106.

The prefix is difficult. The persistent " e " is against Johnston's suggestion " scip here." For the same reason, and because there is no sign of any medial " e," an A.S. * scipera tún, " farm of the shipping folk " is unlikely, though the place is on the Thames. " Shepherd's farm " is more probable, though very doubtful. Dd. forms often omit an " h " and the forms in Kble. and Thorpe above are late copies, perhaps of the twelfth century.

SHERRICK GREEN (Willesden).

   1306.   Scyrewyk (A.D.).

   1307.   Scherewyk (A.D.).

" village or dwelling on the ' scír ' or boundary."

SHOOTUP HILL (Kilburn).

   1604.   Shuttop Hill (quoted Lysons).

   1695.   Suteup Hill (Camden).

   1710.   Seutup Hill (Seller).

Not, I think, to be taken literally. Perhaps a corruption of some personal name ending in -op. Cf. *Allsop, Hartop,* etc., where the -op = the north country local suffix *-hope,* " hollow," " small valley," " access."

SHOREDITCH.
    1216-1307. Soresdych (H.R.).
        1221. Schoresdich (F.F.).
        1235. Schoredich (F.F.).
        1248. Soresdich (F.F.).
        1291. Schoredich (T.E.).
        1457. Shordich (F.F.).
" ditch of Sceorf or * Scorre " (Scorra is in Searle).

Shorwell (I. of W.) was Sorewelle in Dd., Schorewell in T.N., and may contain the weak form *Scorra* as first element.

SHORTWOOD (Staines).
        1754. Short Wood (Rocque).
SIPSON.
        1342. Sibeston (F.F.).
        1391. Sibston (F.F.).
        1394. Sybbiston (A.D.).
        1564. Sybston (F.F.).
        1610. Sypson (Speed).
" farm or enclosure of Sibbe (Sibbi)."

ps > bs > bst. Cf. *Sibson* (Hunts), which has not gone to the further stage of unvoicing the *b* before *s.*

SMITHFIELD.
        1197   Smethefeld   (F.F.).
    1216-1307   (H.R.).
        1272. Smythefeld (F.F.).
        1275   (F.F.).
        1293   Smethefeld   (Escaet).
        1316   (F.A.).
        1535. Smythfeld (V.E.).

"smooth field" (A.S. sméðe).   "Field" in the A.S. sense of
a wide tract of naturally clear open land.

SOUTHALL.

    1210.   Sudhale (R.E.).
    1233.   Suhall (F.F.).
    1261.   Suthalle (F.F.).
    1316.   Suthall (F.A.).
    1496.   Southall (F.F.).
    1695.   Southold (Camden).
    1710.   Southolt (Seller).

"South nook or corner," as opposed to *Northolt* q.v.   In this
case the parasitic *d* or *t* has been dropped again.

SOUTHGATE.

    1371.   Suthgate (A.D.).
    It was the south gate of Enfield Chase.

SPELTHORN (name of a Hundred).

    1086.   Speletorne (Dd.).
    1169, etc.   Spelethorn (P.R.).
    1182.   Spelesthorn (P.R.).
    1200.   Spelethorn (Rot. C.R.).
    1216-1307.   Spellethorn (H.R.).
    1428.   Spelethorn (F.A.).
    1610.   Spelthorne (Speed).

For the suffix, see p. 106.

There is no name Spel or Spel(l)a in Searle.   Perhaps the
prefix is A.S. spel, spell, "story," "discourse," "sermon,"
referring to a certain boundary tree where such was preached
or held.

Cf. *Spelbróc* in Kble., where the prefix (if the form is
genuine) cannot be a personal name.

SPITALFIELDS.

Spyttlefields in 1586 (Ind.), cf. Spitelstrete in 1235 (F.F.). Both named after the priory of St. Mary Spital, founded in 1197.

Spital, Spitel is a M.E. form of old French *ospital*, with a local accenting of the "i" and loss of the first syllable by aphesis.

SPOILBANK WOOD (Hadley).

E.D.D. says: "*spoil bank*, an artificial mound formed of spoil." "*Spoil*, dross, rubbish, surplus soil from an excavation."

STAINES.

‡ 960, 969, 1066. Stana (Kble., Thorpe).
  993. to Stane (Chron.).
  1009. at Stane (Chron.).

1050			(Ind.).
1066	Stane		(Kble.).
1086			(Dd.).
1176	Stanes		(P.R.).
1200			(Rot. C.R.).

Stanes, Staines, subsq.

"at the stone," referring to some boundary mark, perhaps the point where the Colne flows into the Thames.

Prof. Skeat held that the modern (steɪnz) instead of (stoʊnz) was due to Scandinavian influence. See "Place Names of Cambs" under "Staine."

STAMFORD BROOK (Hammersmith).
  1754. Stanford Brook (Rocque).

STAMFORD HILL (Tottenham).
  1321. Staneford (F.F.).

"stony ford."

STANMORE.

1086 }
1213 } Stanmere { (Dd.).
                  { (F.F.).
1230.   Stanmer (F.F.).
1291.   Stanmere (T.E.).
1535.   Stanmer (V.E.).
1710.   Stanmore (Seller).

"stony mere or pool." The 1-inch ordnance map marks three pieces of water in the neighbourhood.

The change of suffix is recent.

STANWELL.

1086.   Stanwelle (Dd.).
1210.   Stanewella (R.E.).
1230.   Stanwell (F.F.).
1281.   Stanewell (Ind.).
1428.   Stanwell (F.A.).

" stony well or spring."

STARVHALL FARM (Drayton).

1862.   Starveall Farm (Ordnance Map).

Names such as this and " Starve acre" seem to imply a poor soil.

STEPNEY.

1086.   Stibenheda (Dd.).
1172.   Stubhuda (P.R.).
1219.   Stibbehe (F.F.).
1216-1307.   Stubeneth (T.N.).
1244 }
1291 } Stebenheth { (F.F.).
                    { (T.E.).
1316.   Stebenhuthe (F.A.).
1353.   Stebenhith (F.F.).
1370.   Stepenhithe (F.F.).
1446.   Stebenheth *alias* Stepney (Escaet).
1535.   Stepenhethe, Stepneth (V.E.).

Stepenhith, Stephenheth, Stepney subsq. Stebenei, Steb-
behe, Stebbenheth, Stubbenhethe, Stebenhithe, etc., in the
F.F. *passim*.

Probably A.S. *Stybban hýð, "hithe of Stybba." See
p. 110 and cf. Stybban snad in Kble. and Bch.

The *e* would be due to Kentish influence, which had e for
A.S. y.

The prefix could not be A.S. stybb, stubb, stebb, "stump,
stub," as that is not a weak noun; nor A.S. stéap, "steep,"
as the forms with "p" do not appear till the fourteenth
century.

For the development of the suffix, cf. *Chelsea* (*supra*) and
Putney, Surrey, Puttenhuthe, Pottenhith, etc., in the Surrey
Fines.

The "n" may have become unvoiced before the "h," which
then caused the "b" to become "p."

* STICKLEDON (Greenford).

> 1331. Stikelynton (F.F.).
> 1373. Stikelyngdon (Escaet).
> 1385. Stikeldon (F.F.).
> 1395. Stekyldon (F.F.).
> 1400. Stykelendon (Escaet).

For the suffix see *don*, p. 100.

The prefix may be A.S. *sticol*, "steep," "lofty," the forms
with "n" being a remnant of the inflected A.S. weak declension, cf. *Hendon*. Doubtful; possibly patronymic of
* Sticol.

STOKE NEWINGTON.

> 1086. Neutone (Dd.).
> 1197. Neweton (F.F.).
> 1286. Newynton (Ch.).
> 1316. Stokneuton (F.A.).

6

1459. Stokenewnton (Ind.).

1535. Newton, Newington, Stokenewington (V.E.).

A.S. æt ðám niwan túne, "at the new farm or enclosure." Cf. *Newnham* (Cambs) and *Newington* (Surrey).

Stoke appears late and cannot be regarded here as an A S. prefix, but was perhaps added merely to distinguish the place from *Newington* (Surrey).

STRAND.

1219. Stranda (F.F.).

1236. la Straunde (F.F.).

1291. la Stronde (T.E.).

etc.

A.S. strand, "margin, edge, shore."

So called, as is well known, because the original village grew up along the bank of the Thames.

STRAND ON THE GREEN (Chiswick).

1353. Stronde (F.F.).

1596. ye Strande (Norden).

1710. Strand Green (Seller).

Cf. preceding.

STROUD GREEN (Hornsey) [strəud].

1562. Strodegrene (F.F.).

1754. Stroud Green (Rocque).

A.S. stród = "marshy land," "marshy land overgrown with brushwood." See supplement to Bosworth's "A.S. Dictionary" and "Transactions of the Philological Society, 1895-1898."

Cf. also Stroud, Strood, Bulstrode, Gostrode, Strudwick, etc., in various counties.

SUDBURY.

1066. Suðbure (Thorpe).

1294. Subyry (F.F.).

1398.   Southbery (Escaet).
1474.   Sutbury (L.I., vol. 16).
1535.   Sudbury (V.E.).

The first element is A.S. suð, "south," which normally becomes *d* before *b*.

For the second element see p. 99.

So called because South of Harrow.

SUNBURY.

     960.   æt Sunnanbyrg (Boh.).
     962.   Sunnanbyrg (Earle, Kble.).
1066.   Sunnabyri (Kble., Thorpe).
1066.   Sunnebyri (Ind.).
1086.   Suneberie (Dd.).
1167.   Sunebia (P.R.).
1258.   Sunnebery (F.F.).
1291.   Sonneber' (T.E.).
1428.   Sonbury (F.A.).
1535.   Sunbury (V.E.).

For the second element see p. 99.

The first element is a personal name *Sunna*, cf. *Sunninghill* (Berks) and *Sunnan dun* (in Kble.).   Also *Sonning*.

*SUTTON (Chiswick).

1221.   Suttone (F.F.).
    1316⎫   ⎧(F.A.)
1327-1377⎬ Sutton ⎨(P.W.).
    1535⎭   ⎩(V.E.).

"south farm or enclosure."   Many places of this name in England.

SUTTON (Hounslow).

Cf. preceding.   Possibly the "Sutton atte Hone," F.F., 1310.

SWAKELEYS (Ickenham).

1327.   Swalclyve (I.M.).
1334.   Swaleclyf (F.F.).
1532.   Swalecliff (F.F.).
1549.   Swalclyf (Ind.).
1695.   Swakley (Camden).
1710.   Swakeleys (Seller).

Not an original Middlesex name, but named after Robert de Swalclyve who held "premises in Herefeld" in 1327. He came from Swalecliff in Kent, which place means " cliff by the Swale river."

I do not know the origin of the Kentish river, but there is another river Swale in Yorks, spelt " Sualua " in Bede. The *l* in Swali- was vocalized between the long vowel and the *k*, and the final *f* being dropped, the spelling of the suffix was assimilated to the common ending -ley. The *s* is modern.

SYON HOUSE (Isleworth).

1414 ⎫   ⎧(Ch.).
1428 ⎬ Syon ⎨(F.A.).
1431 ⎭   ⎩(A.D.).

Sion Abbey was founded by Henry V in 1414, and the name chosen as being an appropriate title for a religious house. Perhaps suggested by the text " Daughters of Sion."

TEDDINGTON.

Type I.
‡ 960, 969.   Tudingtun (Bch., Kble., Thorpe).
     c. 970.   æt Tudincgatunae (Kble.).
     1198.   Tudinton (F.F.).
     1280.   Todinton (F.F.).
     1291.   Todington (T.E.).
     1349.   Tuddyngton (F.F.).
     1443.   Todyngton (F.F.).

    1516.   Todyngton (F.F.).
    1535.   Toddington (V.E.).
    1593.   Tuddington (Ind.).
Type II.
1327-1377.   Tedinton (N.I.).
    1428.   Tedyngton (F.A.).
    1754.   Teddington (Rocque).

Type I. = " farm of the sons of Tuda."

Type II. = " farm of the sons of * Ted(d)a " (unrecorded).

Type II, though the rarer type in M.E. records is the origin of the modern form, which would otherwise have been * Tuddington.

TEMPLE FORTUNE (Hendon).

Marked in Rocque, 1754. I can find no earlier record or history of the place, but the name, if old, suggests that the Knights Templars held land here at one time.

Compare "Robert de Sanford the Master of the Knights Templars in England . . . premises in Hendon and Fynchesl' " (F.F. 1243).

THORNEY (Westminster).

    ‡785.   Torneia (Kble.).
    ‡969.   Thorneye (Bch.).
    ?1042.   þornige (Kble.).
    —1291.   Thorney (T.E.).

" thorn island," " island overgrown with thorns." See p. 106.

* TOLLINGTON (Islington).

    1086.   Tolentone (Dd.).
    1392.   Tolyndon (F.F.).
    1468   ⎫   Tolyngton   ⎧(F.F.).
    1543   ⎭   ⎩(F.F.).
    1710.   Tollington (Seller).

" farm of the sons of Tola " (two in Searle).

TOTHILL (Westminster).

late 12th century.   Tothulle, Totehell (Ind.).
      1257.   Touthull (Cal. Rot. Ch.).
      1268.   Tothull (F.F.).
1480, 1485.   Totehilstrete (F.F.).
      1535.   Totehill (V.E.).

There are other places of this name in England.

It means " look out or spy hill."   M.E. toten, " to spy out " from A.S. totian, " to peep, project."   See also *tout* in N.E.D.

As there is no appreciable natural hill here, the name may have referred to some artificial mound.

The name remains in Tothill Street and the former Tothill fields.

TOTTENHAM.

1086		(Dd.).
1128	Toteham	(Ind.).
1183		(P.R.).
1236.	Thotenham (F.F.).	
1265.	Totenham (F.F.).	
1267		(Ch.).
1286	Tottenham	(F.F.).
1291		(T.E.).
1312	Totenham	(F.F.).
1313		(F.F.).

      Totenham, Tottenham, subsq.

" home or enclosure of Tot(t)a."

Tooting (Surrey) answers to a name *Tōta* with long vowel.

TOTTENHAM COURT.

      1086.   Totehele (Dd.).
    c. 1190 } Totehale { (Ind.).
      1202 } { (F.F.).

1216-1307 } Totenhale { (H.R.).
1303 } { (F.F.).
1347. Totenhal (F.F.).
c. 1510. Totnall Court (L.I., vol. 29).
1596. Totten Court (Norden).
1754. Tottenham Court (Rocque).

"nook or corner of Tot(t)a." Cf. preceding and see p. 102. The gradual change of the suffix may have been due to the influence of "Tottenham," while the *Court* only seems to date from the sixteenth century.

The name remains in the Tottenham Court Road.

TOTTENHAM HALE.

Marked in Rocque. See p. 102.

TOTTENHAM HIGH CROSS.
1551. Totenham Hyghcrosse (F.F.).
1567. Tottenham High Crosse (F.F.).

TURNHAM GREEN.
? 1209. Turneham (Surrey Arch. Soc. Add., vol. I, Surrey Fines).
1596. Turnham Greene (Norden).

It is possible that the 1209 form refers to this place, as there is no place of this name in Surrey.

Histories give no mention of the past of this place, and I can offer no suggestion as to the interpretation of the prefix.

TWICKENHAM.
704. Tuican hom (Bch.).
704. Twican hom (Ind.).
793. Tuicanhamme (Bch.).
1215. Twikeham (F.F.).
1291. Twikenham (T.E.), etc.

The suffix is A.S. hamm, homm, "bend in a river" (Thames). See p. 103.

The prefix is a personal name Twica, rather than A.S. twicen, " crossroads," " meeting of two roads," which would give a modern * *Twichen.*

TWYFORD.

    1086.   Tueverde (Dd.).

    1199 ⎫ Twiford ⎰ (F.F.).
    1291 ⎭   ⎱ (T.E.).

    1380.   Twyford (Escaet), etc.

A.S. twi ford, " double ford," " two fords near together." There are many places of this name in England.

TYBURN.

    971.   andlang Teoburnan (Kble).

    1086.   Tiburne (Dd.).

  1216-1307 ⎫ Tyburn ⎰ (H.R.).
    1235 ⎭   ⎱ (F.F.).

    1299.   Tiburne (F.F.).

    1313.   Teyborn (Rot. Abb.).

    1477.   Tyburn (F.F.).

For the suffix see p.   .

The prefix may be A.S. téah, tíh = " bond," " tie," " fastening "—also " a close," " enclosure," which is probably the meaning here. Cf. Prov. Eng. tye, tighe, " common land," " common pasture."

The spelling in Kble. may be due to the influence of the word *teoh,* " band," " company," which was a related word.

The name *Tyburn* was later superseded by *Marybourne.* (See " Marylebone " (*supra*).

Tey, Tie, Tye are common in Essex local names.

UXBRIDGE.

    1200.   Wxsebrǧe, Oxebrig (Rot. C.R.).

    1202 ⎫ Uxebrigg ⎰ (Rot. Canc.).
    1206 ⎭   ⎱ (F.F.).

1219.   Woxebruge (F.F.).
1220.   Wyxebrigge (F.F.).
1220.   Uxebrugg (Excerpta).
1291.   Woxebregg (T.E.).
1294.   Wexebrigge (Ch.).
1316.   Woxbrigg (F.A.).
1398.   Woxebrigge *als.* Uxbridge (Escaet).
1515.   Uxbrigge (F.F.).
1547.   Wooxbryge (F.F.).
1560.   Uxbridge (F.F.).

The prefix here is rather difficult.   It points to an original *wycs or *wysc, but there is no word like this in A.S.

There is a Celtic root *wysc, *usc = "water," "river," which may be the prefix here, but Celtic names are rare in this part of England, and hence such an origin is extremely doubtful, though the town is certainly situated on the Colne.

The old forms of *Uxendon* (*infra*) seem to point to an unrecorded personal name Wuxa (or Wusca).

Oxen is extremely unlikely, since the old forms all point to an original A.S. *y* or *u*, the *o* in some of the above spellings being of common occurrence for *u* in Norman orthography.

UXENDON FARM (Harrow).

1257.   Woxindon (F.F.).
1310.   Wuxindon (S.S., vol. 19).
1353.   Oxendon (F.F.).
1373.   Woxindon (Close).
1385 }
1394 }   Woxyndon { (F.F.).
(Pat.).
1470.   Woxington (L.I., vol. 16).
1596.   Uxendon (Norden).

For the suffix see p. 100.
The prefix is to be regarded as in the preceding name.

WALBROOK (in the City).

1114-1130 ⎫
1253 ⎪ Walebroc ⎧ (quoted Harben).
1261 ⎬ ⎨ (S.S., vol. 15).
1291 ⎭ ⎩ (Ind.).
(T.E.).
1428. Walbrok (F.A.).

Probably A.S. * Weala brōc, "brook of the foreigners, Britons." Cf. *Walton, Walworth* (Surrey). The latter being " Wealawurð " in 1006 (Kble.).

WALHAM GREEN (Fulham) [wolɔm].

1274, 1280. Wenden (F.F.).
1276, 1284 ⎫ Wanden ⎧ (F.F.).
1312 ⎭ ⎨ (S.S., vol. 33).
1327-1377. Wanden (N.I.).
1481. Wendon (Escaet).
1546. Wanam Grene (F.F.).
1558-1603. Wandon's Green (Proc. Chanc. Eliz.).
1710. Wallam Green (Seller).
1819. Walham Green (Greenwood).

The original suffix was -*den* (see p. 100). It could not, anyway, have been *don* since there is no hill here.

The prefix points to an original * wæn, but there is no such word in A.S., so perhaps one must assume a personal name * Wæna (Wana and Wanna are in Searle). *Wanden* became *Wandam* by dissimilation, then *Wanam*. The change of *n* to *l* is less regular, but occurs sometimes in place names. Cf. Kilburn and Islington. The suffix was then assimilated in spelling to the common terminal -*ham*.

WAPPING.

1231. Wapping (F.F.).
1346. Wappyngge atte Wose (A.D.).
1535. Wapping (V.E.).
1561. Wappinge (F.F.).

Evidently a patronymic.   There is no name Wappa in Searle, but cf. Wappingthorne (in Sussex) which was " *Wappingetorne* " in Dd.

Wose = M.E. wose, " mud," " ooze." 'A.S. wáse.

WAXLOW FARM (Southall).

So spelt in Greenwood, but Wexley in Rocque.   I can find no earlier forms, but it does not appear to be an old name, so far as I can gather from Lysons.

WEALDSTONE (Harrow).

Weald Stone in Rocque 1754.   See *Harrow Weald* (*supra*).
As an inhabited district, quite modern.

WEMBLEY.

825.	æt Wemba lea (Ind., Kble., Thorpe).
1249.	Wambeleg (F.F.).
1508.	Wemley (F.F.).
1535.	Wembley (V.E.).

For the suffix see p. 104.

The prefix may be a personal name * Wæmba—not in Searle, which has, however, two " Wamba " (cf. " Ivanhoe "). This is probable since the form *Wembanlea* is endorsed in a contemporary hand at the end of the 825 A.D. charter.

WESTBOURNE.

1259.	Westeburne (F.F.).
1272-1377.	Westburne (P.W.).
1316.	Westbourn (F.A.).
1754.	Westborn Green (Rocque).

" west bourn or stream "—as opposed to the " Tyburn " to the east.   The village of Westbourn Green lay to the west of Paddington and was absorbed into London, *c.* 1860.

WEST END (Hampstead).

      1535.   Westende (V.E.).

The hamlet lay at the west end of the parish of Hampstead. The name remains in West End Lane.

WEST END (Northolt).

Marked in Rocque.   West end of the parish of Northolt.

WESTMINSTER.

      ‡ 785.   uuestmunstur (Kble.).
      ‡ 804.   uuestmynster (Kble., Thorpe).
      1039.   Westmynster (Chron.).
      1050.   Westmynstre (Chron.).
      1066.   Westmenstre (Thorpe).
      1199.   Westminster (F.F.).
      1305.   Westmonastre (Escaet).

A.S. "*mynster*" was early borrowed from Latin "*monasterium*."

Westminster lay to the west of the City of London.

WHETSTONE.

      1466.   Whetston (F.F.).
      1490.   Wheston (L.I., vol. 20).
      1516.   Whetstone (F.F.).
      1535.   Westone (V.E.).

  1558-1603.   Whetston *alias* Fryern (Proc. Chanc. Eliz.).

Probably simply "at the whetstone," but one cannot say for certain without earlier forms.

Whetstone (Leicester) was Westan in 1250 (Ind.), Whetestan, Wetstan, Westan in 1318, 1340 (Ch.), Wetyston, Weitston in 1300 (F.A.), and means undoubtedly what it says.

W. is on the Great North Road.

WHITECHAPEL.
    1348.   Whitechapele (F.F.).
    1359.   Whitchapelle (F.F.).
    1363.   Whitechapel in Algatestrete (F.F.).
    1377.   la Whytechapel without Algate (A.D.).

WHITEHEATH FARM (Harefield).
    1819.   White Heath Farm (Greenwood).

WHITTON (Hounslow).
    1300.   Witton (Escaet).
    1354.   Whitton (F.F.).
 1357, 1437.   Whytton (F.F.).
    1535.   Whitton (V.E.).
" white farm or enclosure."

The long vowel in A.S. *hwīt* is usually shortened in composition, when it occurs as a first element in place names.

WILLESDEN (wɪlzdɔn).
   ‡939.   Wellesdune (Kble.).
    1086.   Wellesdone (Dd.).
    1180.   Wilesdune (Ind.).
    1248.   Wullesdon (F.F.).
    1277.   Wyllesdon (F.F.).
    1291.   Willesdon (T.E.).
    1316.   Wyllesdon (F.A.).
    1563.   Wylsdon (F.F.).
    1710.   Wilsdon, Wilsdon Green (Seller).

The original suffix was *don* (see p. 100), and the change to *den* must be quite recent.

The prefix is a personal name " Wille " (or rather " Wylle "), not actually in Searle, but the weak form " Willa " occurs, short for one of the A.S. personal names beginning with *Wil-*.

The earliest forms above rather favour an A.S. y, for which *u* is a Norman and *e* a Kentish spelling.

WINCHMORE HILL.

       1319.   Wynsemerhull (A.D.).

       1543.   Wynsmore hill (F.F.).

       1565.   Wynsmorehill (F.F.).

       1596.   Winchmore Hill (Norden).

" hill at the boundary of Wynsige."

    The late form *Winsi* is noted in Searle.

    A.S. *gemǣru*, " boundary," is more likely to be corrupted to " mor " than *mere*, " mere."

WOODEND (Northolt and Hayes).

   (Hayes) 1531.   Wodehende (F.F.).

(Northolt) 1674.   Woodend (Ind.).

WOOD GREEN (Hornsey).

 1695, 1710.   Wood-Green (Camden, Seller).

    It was a hamlet at the edge of the great wood of Tottenham.

WOODHALL (Pinner).

   1327-1377 $\Big\}$ Wodehalle $\begin{cases} \text{(N.I.).} \\ \text{(F.F.).} \end{cases}$
       1332

       1349 $\left. \begin{array}{} \\ \\ \\ \\ \end{array} \right\}$ Wodhall $\begin{cases} \text{(F.F.).} \\ \text{(F.F.).} \\ \text{(Escaet).} \\ \text{(F.F.).} \end{cases}$
       1354
       1378
       1415

    For the suffix see p. 102.

WOODSIDE (Finchley).

       1710 Wood Side (Seller).

WORMHOLT, " WORMWOOD SCRUBBS."

       1200.   Wermeholte (Rot. C.R.).

       1290.   Wrmeholt (I.p.m.).

       1465.   Wormholt (L.I., vol. 5).

1819.   Wormholt farm.   Wormholt Scrubbs (Green-
              wood).
1862.   Wormholt farm.   Wormwood Scrubbs (6-inch.
              Ordnance map).

For the suffix see p. 104.

The prefix is a personal name Wyrma, short for one of the A.S. names beginning with *Wyrm*, "dragon," "snake."

Scrubbs = "brushwood," "underwood," "waste land over-grown with low shrubs and bushes."

"The piece of land called Wormholt Common or Scrubs was formerly a wood containing about 200 acres, about sixty of which have been enclosed" (Lysons).

WORTON HALL (Hounslow).

1357			F.F.
1375	} Worton {		(Close).
1422			(F.F.).
1449			(A.D.).
1535.	Wortton (V.E.).		

Probably A.S. *wyrt tún*, "herb enclosure," "kitchen garden."

WROTHAM PARK (Mimms).

Called after Wrotham in Kent, the ancient residence of the family of Admiral Byng, who built the Middlesex place *c.* 1754.

YEADING (jedɪŋ).

‡727	} Geddinges {	(Ind.).
‡757		(Bch., Kble.).
825.	æt Geddincggum (Bch., Kble., Thorpe).	
1210.	Geddinges (R.E.).	
1325.	Yeddinggs (F.F.).	
1338.	Yedding (F.F.).	
1710.	Yeding (Seller).	

" place of the sons of Gedd or Geddi."   Johnston compares the surname *Giddings*, but this would answer rather to a name *Gydda*, the *g* remaining before A.S. y.

YEOVENEY FARM (Staines) [jʋː v].

1219.   Yveneye (F.F.).
1251.   Iveneye (I.M.).
1272-1377.   Yveneye (P.W.).
1383.   Yeveneye (F.F.).
1535.   Yeveney (V.E.).
1695.   Eveney (Camden).
1819.   Yeovenny (Greenwood).

For the second element see p. 101.

The first element is a personal name * Gēfa.   *Gyfa* is in Searle, but the *g* sound would remain before A.S. y.

YIEWSLEY (juː zlɪ).

1383.   Wyveslee (F.F.).
1504, 1516.   Wyvesley (F.F.).
1596.   Wewesley (Norden).
1819.   Yewsley (Greenwood).

Prefix is a personal name * Wif or perhaps Wifel.   The *v* here became *w* and the initial consonant was then dropped before the sound [ʋː u, jː u].   A.S. *wif* (wife, woman) seems less likely but is possible.

ADDENDUM.

MAYFAIR.

1709.   " Reasons for suppressing the yearly fair in Brookfield. Westminster, commonly called May Fair."   (Quoted from Clinch's " History of Mayfair and Belgravia.")

The fair here was granted by James II. in 1688, to be held in May.

ADDENDA.

I. List of a Few Local Names on the 1-Inch Ordnance Map, of Obvious Meaning, and Probably Fairly Modern.

> *Broadwater Farm* (Harefield).
> *Hill Farm* (Ickenham).
> *Hillend* (Harefield).
> *Hollyhill Farm* (Enfield).
> *Hundred Acres Farm* (Northolt).
> *Kentonlane Farm* (Kenton).
> *Longlane Farm.*
> *Low Farm* (Hanworth).
> *Newpond Farm* (Ruislip).
> *Newyears Green* (Harefield).
> *Oak Farm* (Hillingdon).
> *Shepherdshill Farm* (Harefield).
> *Valley Farm* (Kingsbury).
> *Warren Farm* (Uxbridge).
> *Windmill Hill* (Ruislip).
> *Woodcock Hill* (Harefield and Harrow).

II. List of Some Extinct Middlesex Place Names, Chiefly from the F.F.

Bradeford, 1207, *F.F. Bradfordbrige*, F.F., 1532. In St. Pancras parish. Can the later "Battlebridge" be a corruption of this?

Cleremont, F.F., 1535. *Cleremondes*, F.F., 1544. Near Staines. I suppose a Norman name, " clear or bright hill."

Dermodeswell, F.F., 1247, " well or spring of Dēormōd."

Fackeswell, F.F., 1197, " well or spring of Fac(c)." (Facca is in Searle.)

Farncroft, F.F., 1197, " fern croft or paddock." In Stepney.

Fiscesburna, Ind., 704, " stream of Fisc."

Frith (a wood called . . . in Edelmeton), F.F., 1205. M.E. *frith*, " a wood." See *Frith Manor* (*supra*).

Herefreðing lond (near Harrow ??). Ind., Kble. and Thorpe, 825, " land of the sons of Herefrið."

Kingisholte, F.F., 1253, " kings wood."

Lullinges tréo, Ind., 704, " tree of the son of Lulla."

Nanesmaneslande (Dd.). Nonemanneslond, 1255 (Ind.), " no man's land," " land without ownership."

Ravenyngemyll, F.F., 1404, " mill of the sons of Raven." (A.S. hræfn). Early in use as a personal name.

Reye, next Feltham, F.F., 1294 ; Reye, F.F., 1305. ? A.S. riðe. M.E. rithe, ride, rie " small stream."

Rudynge, F.F., 1318 ; *la Rudinge*, F.F., 1326 ; *Rudyng*, F.F., 1349, 1365. Looks like a patronymic, " place of the sons of Rūda."

Skinnereswell, F.F., 1197, " well of Skinner," i.e. the skinner.

Wenmaresfeld (. . . in Edelmeton), F.F., 1205, " field or clear space of * Wēnmære."

Wulvesfeld, F.F., 1205, " field or clear space of Wulf."

III. MIDDLESEX RIVERS AND STREAMS.

The Colne, Lea, and Thames merely form the W., E. and S. boundaries of the county and are not true Middlesex streams.

Ashe or Exe. See Ashford.

Brent. See Brentford.

Crane. Back formation from Cranford.

Fleet. See *Fleet.*

Holborn. See *Holborn.*

Pimmes Brook, probably called after a man Pim(m).

Pin. Back formation from Pinner.

Tyburn, Westbourn, Walbrook (q.v.).

Yeading Brook. See *Yeading.*

IV. NOTE ON THE SUFFIXES TO MIDDLESEX NAMES.

-BURY.

bury comes from A.S. byrig, dative case of burh—" stronghold," " defended spot," " fortified place "—from the frequent use of the preposition *æt* ("at") before place names, which governed the dative case.

The nominative *borough* is unknown in Middlesex, and the majority of places with the suffix *-bury* date from M.E. or very late A.S. times, when the distinction between *borough* and *bury* was lost.

Prof. Mawer informs me that " bury " as a suffix to Middlesex, Herts and Essex names came to be used with little more than the sense of " manor." This, I suppose, refers to those names of post-conquest origin.

Aldermanbury, Barnsbury, Bloomsbury, Brondesbury, Bucklersbury, Canonbury, Ebury, Finsbury, Gunnersbury, Highbury, Kingsbury, Lothbury, Sudbury, Sunbury.

-BOURN, -BURN.

A.S. *burna,* " stream," " brook," " running water."

Bourn Farm, Holborn, Kilburn, Marylebone, Tyburn, Westbourn.

-BRIDGE.

A.S. brycg. M.E. brigge, brygge, brugge, bregge (Kentish).

Knightsbridge, Uxbridge.

7 *

-BROOK.

A.S. brōc, "brook," "rushing stream."   M.E. brok, broke.
Only in *Walbrook*.

-CHURCH.

A.S. cyrice, cyrce.   M.E. chirche, churche, cherche.
Only in the City Churches : *Abchurch, Fenchurch, Grace-church*.

-CLIFF.

A.S. clif.
Only in *Ratcliff*, "Swakeleys" being an imported name.

-COTE.

A.S. *cot* (neut.) and *cote* (fem.), "dwelling," "house,"
"cottage."   "Originally the word had a general sense, and
if applied to a man's house, did not necessarily imply a
humble abode" (Prof. Wyld, "Place Names of Lancs,"
p. 312).
Chalk Farm, Eastcote, Knightscote, Sheepcote.

-DEN.

A.S. *denu*, "valley," "dell."   M.E. dene, den.
(?) *Walham Green.*

-DITCH.

A.S. *dic*, "ditch," "dike."
Houndsditch, Shoreditch.

-DON.

A.S. dūn, "hill," "down"—perhaps sometimes "fortified
hill," of Celtic origin (see N.E.D.), and the same word as
Modern English "down," but unstressed.
*Down Barnes, Hendon, Hillingdon, Horsendon, Islington,
Neasden, (?) Stikeldon, Uxendon, Willesden.*

-END.

A.S. *ende*, "end." Hence "a limit," "boundary," "border." Common in Middlesex names, generally as a detached word.

Crouch End, Hatch End, Kings End, Kitts End, Mile End, Ponders End, West End (2), *Wood End.*

-EY.

A.S. *ēʒ, iēʒ,* "island." The word was also used to denote a tract of elevated land, wholly or partly surrounded by low marshy ground. There was also an A.S. *ēa,* "water river," "stream," which may have influenced the A.S. *ēʒ* in place names.

Eye, Hackney, Hornsey (?), *Thorney, Yeoveney.*
As prefix in *Ebury.*

-FIELD.

A.S. *feld* meant not so much "field" in the modern sense, as "tract of open land opposed to woodland," "stretch of unenclosed land for pasture or grazing."

Enfield, Harefield, Smithfield, Spitalfields (late).
(?) as prefix in *Feltham* (doubtful).

-FOLD.

A.S. *fald, falod,* "fold or pen for sheep, etc."
Only in *Old Fold.*

-FONT.

See *Bedfont.*

-FORD.

A.S. *ford,* "a ford." Cognate with Latin *portus.*
Ashford, Brentford, Cranford, Dernford, Greenford, Halliford, Hodford, Longford, Old Ford, Sandford, Stamford, Twyford.

-FRITH, -FLEET. See *Frith* and *Fleet.*

-GATE.

A.S. *geat*, "gate," "opening," "passage." Distinct from O.N. *gata*, "road," "way."

The modern form with *g* instead of *y* is generally attributed to the influence of the plural *gatu*.

Highgate, Oxgate, Southgate, and the "City" gates.

-GORE. See *Gore*.

-GREEN.

N.E.D. says: "A piece of public or common grassy land, situated in or near a town or village, from which it often takes its name."

E.D.D. says: "A common, open or waste piece of ground."

Common in Middlesex names as a detached word.

Bethnal Green, Golders Green, Goulds Green, Palmers Green, Parsons Green, Turnham Green, Walham Green, Wood Green, etc.

-HALE.

The A.S. "*healh*" (dative "*heale*"). Old Mercian "halh, hale" meant "a nook, corner, retreat." It is often difficult to tell in place names whether this word or A.S. heall, M.E. halle (= "hall") is implied, since both may occur as *hall(e)*, though one "l" is the regular form for A.S. *healh*. Doubtless the M.E. *halle* was often substituted for an older *hale*, when the latter became obsolete as a living word.

Bethnal, Copthall, Frognal, Hale, Kensal (??), Moorhall, Northolt, Ruckhold (?), Southall, "Tottenham Court," Tottenham Hale, Woodhall.

E.D.D. gives a more modern dialectal meaning: "Flat alluvial land by the side of a river," which would suit the situation of *Tottenham Hale* by the flat meadow land beside the Lea,

-HAM.

May represent :—

1. A.S. *hám*, "home," "dwelling," "enclosure."

2. A.S. *hamm, homm*, "enclosure," "piece of land enclosed or hemmed in," "plot of meadow or pasture land."

3. A.S. *hamm, homm*, "piece of land enclosed in the bend of a river," i.e. shaped like the bend of the knee ["ham"].

1. *Astleham, Feltham (?), Ickenham, Laleham, Tottenham.*

2. *Colham (?).*

3. *Fulham, Twickenham.*

-HANGER.   See *Hanger Hill, Pitshanger.*

-HARROW.   See *Harrow.*

-HATCH.

A.S. *hæc* (half-door, wicket) ; M.E. *hacche.*   Often referring to the side gate of some estate or enclosure.

Colney Hatch.   Hatch End.

-HEATH.   A.S. *hǽð.*

Cambridge Heath, Heathrow (?), Peel Heath, Whiteheath (late).

-"HESE."   See *Hayes, Heston.*

-HILL.

A.S. *hyll.*   M.E. hylle, hulle, hille, helle (Kentish), etc.

Common in Middlesex, but generally as a detached word, and chiefly in modern names.

Chalkhill, Chattern Hill, Childs Hill, Clayhill, Cornhill, Dancershill, Dollishill, Greenhill, Hangerhill, Highwood Hill, Mill Hill, Polehill, Red Hill, Shootup Hill, Tothill, Winchmore Hill.

-HITHE.   See *Chelsea, Stepney.*

-HOLT.

A.S. *holt*, "a wood, copse."
Only in *Wormholt*.

-HOOK.

A.S. *hōc*, "hook," hence "projecting point of land."
Pentonhook.

-HOUSE.

A.S. *hús*.   M.E. hous, hows.
Cowhouse.

-HIDE, -HYDE.   See *Hyde, North Hyde*.

-ING.

This suffix was used in A.S. as a patronymic, attached to a
personal name, the sense being " the son(s) or descendant(s)
of."
The declension in A.S. was :—

		Singular.	*Plural.*
Nom. Acc.		-ing	-ingas
	Gen.	-inges	-inga
	Dat.	-inge	-ingum

1. *Alone : Charing, Ealing, Notting, Wapping, Yeading.*
2. "*-ingdon.*"   *Hillingdon* (for meaning here, see under
Hillingdon).
3. *-ington : Charlton, Harlington, Kempton, Kensington,
Kenton, Oakington, Paddington, Teddington, Tollington.*

-LAND.   See *Kingsland*.

-LEY.

A.S. lēah (dative lēage) = " tract of cultivated or cultivable
land," "piece of land cleared from forest for pasture, etc."
The general meaning seems to have been, " land artificially
cleared " as opposed to *feld* (q.v.), which meant, "land naturally clear and open."

Bentley, Brockley, Cowley, Dawley, Eversley, Finchley, Hadley, Osterley, Wembley, Yiewsley.

-LIP. See *Ruislip.*

-LOW.

A.S. *hlǣw,* M.E. lawe, lowe, " mound," " tumulus "—also " rising ground."   Only in *Hounslow.*

-MERE.

A.S. *mere,* " mere," " pool," " pond."
Rugmere (?), *Stanmore.*

-MINSTER. See *Westminster.*

-MYTHE. See *Hammersmith.*

-OAST. See *Limehouse.*

-ORA, -ER. See *Pinner.*

-POOL.

A.S. pōl, " pool."
Portpool.

" **-SEAð.**" See *Roxeth,* cf. Prov. Eng. " sheath," a brine pit.

-STEAD.

A.S. *stede,* " place," " stead."   In Middlesex only in the combination *hám stede,* " homestead "—*Hampstead.*

-STONE.

A.S. *stán,* " stone "—often some boundary stone.
Haggerston, Ossulston, Staines.

-STREET.

E.D.D. says : " a hamlet or few scattered cottages."
The name occurs in all the Home Counties—generally in small hamlets.
Perhaps referred originally to a little row of houses

growing up alongside an already existing road or way, as opposed to a straggling village.

Bury Street, Green Street, Mare Street, Page Street.

-STRAND. See *Strand*.

-STROUD. See *Stroud*.

-THORN.

A.S. *þorn*, " thorn," " thorn tree." Probably used to denote boundaries or landmarks when occurring in place names.

Elthorne, Spelthorn.

-TON.

A.S. *tún*, " enclosure "—hence, " farmhouse," " settlement," " farmstead with its outbuildings."

For the development in meaning of modern English " town," cf. Latin *villa* and French *ville*.

This is the commonest suffix to place names in England as a whole, and examples in Middlesex are very numerous.

Acton, Alperton, Boston, Brompton, Charlton, Clapton, Dalston, Drayton, Edmonton, Hampton, Harlesden, Harlington, Hatton, Headstone (?), Heston, Homerton, Hoxton, Kempton, Kensington, Kenton, Kentish Town, Lampton, Lisson, Littleton, Norton, Oakington, Paddington, Preston, Shepperton, Sipson, Stoke Newington, Teddington, Tollington, Whitton, Worton.

-VALE. See *Perivale*.

-WALL. A.S. *weall, Blackwall*.

-WARE. See *Edgeware*.

-WAY. *Holloway*.

-WEALD. *Harrow Weald*.

-WELL.

A.S. welle, wielle, etc., " spring," " source," " well,"
The word was used as often of a natural spring as of an
artificial well.

*Botwell, Clerkenwell, Goswell, Haliwell, Hanwell, Muswell,
Pinkwell (?), Shaklewell, Shadwell, Stanwell.*

-WICK.

A.S. *wic,* " dwelling," " house," " village." It is a disputed
question whether this word is native or merely borrowed
from the Latin *uicus.* O.N. *vik,* " creek," " bay," is unre-
lated.

*Aldwich, Chiswick, Hackney Wick, Hampton Wick, Hali-
wick, Pallingswick.*

-WOOD.

A.S. wudu. M.E. wode, wude, " wood," " forest."
*Cricklewood, Highwood Hill, Ken Wood, Northwood, Nor-
wood, St. John's Wood, Short Wood (?).*
As prefix in : *Wood Green, Woodhall, Woodside.*

-WORTH.

A.S. weorþ, wurþ, wyrþ, " enclosure," " farm," " estate,"
" holding," " homestead with surrounding land."
Prof. Skeat considered the word to be related to A.S. weorþ
= " worth " (of value).
Hanworth, Harmondsworth, Isleworth, Rudsworth.

Miscellaneous Names.

(1) *Bayswater, Belsize, Bow, Cockfosters, Coldharbour,
Mimms, Perry Oaks, Pontefract, Poplar, Shepherds Bush,
Spoilbank, Whetstone.*

V. Note on the Prefixes to Middlesex Names.

A. *Personal Prefixes.*

A.S. personal names may be divided into two classes, as far as declension is concerned—those ending in *a* and those ending in any other vowel or a consonant.

Those in *a* formed their genitive singular in *-an*, the others in *-es*.

Most names ending in *a* were really shortened or "pet" (to use Prof. Skeat's word) forms of some longer name. Thus *Billa* was short for some name like *Bilfrith, Bilheard, Bilhelm,* etc. (A.S. *bil,* "a sword").

ABBA	*Abchurch.* Cf. surname "Abbs."
ALA, ALLA	*Aldgate.*
ÆCG, ÆCGE	*Edgeware.* A.S. *Ecg,* "sword" (lit. "edge").
ÆLLA	*Elthorne.* Name of the conqueror of Sussex.
ÆNA	*Enfield.*
BEDA	*Bedfont.* Cf. "the Venerable Bede."
BILLA	*Billingsgate,* Bil. A.S. *bil,* "sword."
BOTA	*Botwell.*
BRAND	*Brondesbury.*
* CEARRA	*Charing.*
* CEARDA, CERDA	*Charlton.*
CENEBRIHT (?)	*Cambridge Heath,* "bold, bright."
CENA, CŒNA	*Kempton, Kenton.* A.S. *céne,* "bold" "brave" ("keen").
CYNESIGE (?)	*Kensington,* "bold victory."
CNOTTA	*Notting.*
CŪFA	*Cowley.*
CYNA (?)	*Kilburn.* Cynebriht, beald, heard, etc.
DEORLAF	*Dalston.*

* Dūfa	*Dowgate.*
Eadhelm	*Edmonton,* " happy helmet."
Ealdræd	*Aldersgate,* " old counsel."
Ealhperht	*Alperton.* Cf. " Albert."
Eastulf (?)	*Astleham* (east + wolf)
* Eccel, Æccel	*Ashford.* Cf. surname *Eccles.*
Fin(n)	*Finsbury.*
* Finc	*Finchley,* " finch."
Gedd(i)	*Yeading.* Not related to surname " *Geddes.*"
Gill(us)	*Ealing.*
* Gistel (?)	*Isleworth.*
Gōda	*Goswell,* " good."
Gunhild(a)	*Gunnersbury,* a feminine name.
Gēfa	*Yeoveney.*
Haca	*Hackney.*
Heahmær	*Hammersmith.*
Hana	*Hanwell, Hanworth,* " cock."
Hara (??)	*Hornsey,* " hare."
Head(d)a	*Hadley.*
Heregod, Heregold	*Haggerston.* A.S. here = " army."
Heremōd	*Harmondsworth,* " army courage."
Here(w)ulf	*Harlesden,* " army wolf."
Hlōþa	*Lothbury.*
Hocc, Hocg	*Hoxton.* Cf. surname *Hogg* > Hocga.
Hod(a)	*Hodford.* Cf. surname *Hodding.*
Horsa	*Horsendon,* " mare."
Hrōc	*Ruckhold (?), Roxeth,* " rook."
Hunbeorht	*Homerton.* Cf. names " Hubert," " Humbert."
Hund	*Hounsditch, Hounslow,* " dog."
Hygeræd (?)	*Harlington,* " mind counsel."
Lil(le)	*Lisson.*

LYTEL	*Littleton,* " little."
[MIMMAS or MIMMAN	*Mimms.* ? a small tribe or family.]
OSWULF	*Ossulston,* " god wolf."
PAD(D)A	*Paddington.* ? Celtic name [initial " p."]
PALLIG, PALLINGUS (??)	*Pallingswick.* ? Danish.
PINCA (?)	*Pinkwell.* ? Celtic = " finch."
PINNA	*Pinner.*
PURTA	*Portpool.*
RUDDA	*Rudsworth.*
* SCEACUL (?)	*Shacklewell.* ? " shackle."
* SCEORRE, SCEORF (?)	*Shorditch.*
SIB, SIBBE	*Sipson.*
STYBBA (?)	*Stepney.*
SUNNA	*Sunbury,* short for some name *Sun-* [A.S. *sunne,* " sun "].
TICCA	*Ickenham.*
TID(W)ULF	*Elstree.*
TŌCA	*Oakington.*
TOLA	*Tollington.*
TOTA	*Tottenham.*
TUD(D)A	*Teddington.*
* TURNA (??)	*Turnham Green.*
TWICA	*Twickenham.*
* WAPA	*Wapping.*
* WÆMBA	*Wembley.*
* WÆNA (??)	*Walham Green.*
WĪNESIGE	*Winchmore.*
* WĪFE, WĪFEL	*Yiewsley.*
WILLE, * WYLLE	*Willesden,* short for some name Wil-.
WYRMA	*Wormholt,* short for some name Wyrm-.

Norman or Post Conquest Names.

Baignard	*Bayswater.*
Bernier	*Barnsbury.*
Bleomund (?)	*Bloomsbury.*
Breakspear	*Breakspears.* ("Brake spere.")
Bruce	*Bruce Castle.*
Bukerell	*Bucklersbury.*
Clitheroe	*Clutterhouse.* ("Cliderhou.")
Hamond	*Hammonds Farm.* ("Haman.")
Hercy	*Hercies Farm.*
Peachey	*Cowley Peachey.* ("Pecche.")
Poille, Puille, Poyle	*Poyle.*

and quite modern names—*Child, Cubitt, Dancer, Dolley, Golder, Gould, Page, Penton, Peel, Pimlico, Ponder, Potter, Shepherd,* etc.

B. Prefixes other than Personal Names.

1. *Animals,* etc.

brock (badger).	*Brockley.*
cow	*Cowhouse.*
crane	*Cranford.*
frog (? ?)	*Frogmore, Frognal.*
lamb	*Lampton.*
ox	*Oxgate.*
sheep	*Sheepcote.*

2. *Plants,* etc.

ash (?)	*Ashford.*
bent-grass	*Bentley.*
bramble	*Bromley.*
broom	*Brompton.*
corn	*Cornhill.*
grass	*Gracechurch.*
moss	*Muswell.*

OAK	*Acton.*
PEAR TREE	*Perivale, Perry Oaks.*
POPLAR	*Poplar.*
RUSH	*Ruislip.*
THORN	*Thorney* (Elthorn, Spel- thorn).
" WORT " (herb)	*Worton.*

3. *Soil,* etc.

CHALK	*Chalkhill, Chelsea.*
CLAY	*Clay Hill.*
FEN ‧	*Fenchurch.*
HEATH	*Heathrow, Hatton.*
IRON (?)	*Islington.*
LIME	*Limehouse.*
SAND	*Sandford.*
STONE	*Stamford, Stanmore, Stan- well.*

4. *Rank,* etc.

ALDERMAN	*Aldermanbury.*
BISHOP	*Bishopsgate.*
CANON	*Canonsbury.*
" CLERK "	*Clerkenwell.*
CRIPPLE (?)	*Cripplegate.*
FRIARS	*Friern Barnet.*
" HALLOW " (saint)	*Halliford.*
" HERE " (army)	*Harefield.*
KING	*Kingsbury.*
KNIGHT	*Knightsbridge, Knightscote.*
PRIEST	*Preston.*
" WEALH " (foreigner, Briton)	*Walbrook.*

5. *Various.*

CHEESE	*Chiswick.*
" CLOP "	*Clapton.*

" CRICKLE "	*Cricklewood* (q.v.).
CROUCH	*Crouch End.*
" DOLE "	*Dawley.*
" DRAY "	*Drayton.*
A.S. EOWISTRE (?)	*Osterley.*
FELT (?)	*Feltham.*
HEDGE	*Headstone.*
HOLLOW, HOLE	*Holborn, Holloway.*
A.S. LÆL (?)	*Laleham.*
MILL	*Mill Hill.*
MOOR	*Moorhall.*
" NESE "	*Neasden.*
" SPELL "	*Spelthorn.*
" TOUT "	*Tothill.*
" TY " (tie)	*Tyburn.*
" UX " (wysc, wycs)	*Uxbridge.*

6. *Adjectives.*

BLACK	*Blackwall.*
BLITHE (?)	*Bethnal Green.*
" COPPED " (i.e. pollarded)	*Copthall.*
EAST	*Eastcote.*
FULL (?)	*Fulham.*
GREEN	*Greenford, Greenhill, Green Street.*
HIGH	*Hendon, Highbury, Highgate, Highwood.*
" KENTISH "	*Kentish Town.*
LITTLE	*Littleton.*
LONG	*Longford.*
NEW	*Stoke Newington.*
NORTH	*Northolt, North Hyde, Northwood, Norton Folgate, Norwood Green.*

OLD	*Aldwich, Old Fold, Old Ford.*
RED	*Ratcliff.*
SHALLOW	*Shadwell.*
SMOOTH	*Smithfield.*
SOUTH	*Southall, Southgate, Sudbury, Sutton.*
TWO (i.e. double)	*Twyford.*
WEST	*Westbourne, West End, Westminster.*
WHITE	*Whitechapel, Whitton.*

PRINTED IN GREAT BRITAIN BY THE UNIVERSITY PRESS, ABERDEEN

Lightning Source UK Ltd.
Milton Keynes UK
UKOW01f1213040813

214802UK00002B/109/P